Astonished by the Word

Reading Scripture For
Deep Transformation

Brian D. Russell

Astonished by the Word: Reading Scripture for Deep Transformation

Copyright 2023 by Brian D. Russell

This book is printed on acid-free, elemental chlorine-free paper.

ISBN: Paperback 978-1-953495-73-0, eBook 978-1-953495-74-7

23 24 25 26 27 28 29 —10 9 8 7 6 5 4 3 2 1

MANUFACTURED in the UNITED STATES of AMERICA

To my parents, Dale and Midge Russell, for reading Scripture together as a couple and attending a church that taught the Holy Scriptures faithfully. I learned to value the Bible from childhood because you did.

Contents

Acknowledgments

No book writes itself. *Astonished by the Word* represents my current thinking about the study of Scripture. I am grateful for the privilege of teaching over a thousand students in various courses about Old and New Testament interpretation at Asbury Theological Seminary since 2000. Teaching is never a one-way conversation. I've learned much from the feedback and rich discussions in class, private conversations with students, and in spiritual formation groups. Moreover, I recognize the privilege of the academic life for having time to read and reflect upon not only the Bible but on the processes involved in studying it deeply. I wrote a significant portion of the initial draft of this book while on a sabbatical leave from Asbury during fall 2020.

I am also grateful for Invite Resources for publishing this manuscript. Thank you, Len Wilson, and your outstanding team. You all have been a pleasure to work with.

Finally, thank you to my family for your ongoing love and support. Love is first and foremost lived out in community with those closest to you, and I am blessed. Astrid: Our spiritual partnership has been the foundation for my growth now for over a decade. Micaela and Katrina: My desire to model love for God and neighbor for you continues to inspire me. Julio, Nana, Pati, and Sarah: Learning to be the stepfather you deserve has taught me much about the blind spots in my growth in love, and I'm a better man because you are in my life.

Introduction

······●······

In *On Christian Teaching*, Augustine writes, "So anyone who thinks that he has understood the divine scriptures or any part of them but cannot by his understanding build up this double love of God and neighbor, has not yet succeeded in understanding them."[1]

In other words, the goal of biblical interpretation is the ongoing conversion of the Bible's readers into persons who love God and others. Most of us likely desire this transformation. We want to grow in grace. We want to live out of wholeness. We want to be perfected in love so that we can live fully as the people God created us to be.

We also understand that being filled with love is central to the work of the Holy Spirit in our lives. In Romans 5:5, Paul writes in part, "God's love has been poured into our hearts through the Holy Spirit that has been given to us." In Galatians 5:22–23, Paul lists the fruits of the Spirit as love, joy, peace, patience, kindness, generosity, faithfulness, gentleness, and

---

1   Augustine, *On Christian Teaching*, *Oxford World's Classics* (Oxford: Oxford University Press, 1997), 27.

self-control. Arguably, love is the principal fruit, and the others are different facets of the active expression of love.

I want to explore a process of reading Scripture for growth in the love of God and neighbor. Augustine's model seems simple. It almost seems too obvious for comment. But it is not easy to implement at the core of our being. At least, it hasn't been easy for me. If it were easy, we would not witness the ongoing failures of many Christ followers to uphold the character of Jesus. Likewise, we would not see the struggles of the Church especially in the formerly Christian West to reach emerging generations with the Gospel. Too many people equate Christians with hate and exclusion rather than love and inclusion.

Yet the Bible offers us a world in which God has created a holy people for himself for the sake of the world. How is it that sometimes Scripture appears ineffective in creating a deep transformation that allows the Church consistently to be known by love?

From my personal experience as well as my engagement with students, pastors, and spiritual leaders, I believe that one of the principal obstacles to achieving Augustine's vision is our inability to move past our biases, blind spots, and unconscious blocks. We may read Scripture, but I wonder if we allow it to read us? Are we really open to the work that God desires to do in us through the words of the Bible?

Most of us would instinctively say, "Yes." But the true mark of openness to Scripture is how we respond to those parts of the Bible that question our way of life rather than someone else's.

Humans have always suffered from blind spots. Our ability to establish boundaries and recognize patterns is critical to the establishment of distinct networks, institutions, and nations. But our ability to organize and sort information creates the illusion that we *see* reality accurately. The truth is as Paul wrote, "For now we see in a mirror, dimly" (1 Cor 13:12). A popular anonymous saying teaches, "We see the world not as it is but as we are." Not only do our blinders distort our ability to perceive the world around us but our blind spots also challenge the accuracy of our self-understanding. Gerald May wrote, "How we view ourselves at any given time may have very little to do with how we really are."[2]

Our brains have the powerful ability to organize and sort an array of sensory data. We can recognize patterns. We create rules and assumptions that allow us to act quickly and unconsciously. Let me illustrate with a common experience to which I trust you can relate. I remember when I purchased a blue Hyundai Sonata in 2011. As soon as I drove off the lot, I began noticing all of the other Sonatas on the roads of central Florida. Before buying, I don't recall seeing many of them, but once I owned a Sonata, they seemed to be everywhere.

What if these same blind spots, biases, and unconscious blocks are present whenever we read the Bible? What might we be missing simply because our eyes and ears are trained to *see* and *hear* only certain truths and to pass over or ignore others?

One of the most difficult biases is the fear of being wrong. We can easily get to a point where we *think* or *feel* that we grasp the Gospel. Then we approach the Bible for affirmation about

---

2   Gerald G. May, *Addiction and Grace : Love and Spirituality in the Healing of Addictions* (San Francisco: HarperOne, 2007), 172.

what we already know rather than for even deeper growth in love. Charles Williams observed, "There must be . . . something of that intellectual willingness to be wrong in order that words may be heard? Thus, people can never read the Bible for either they believe it, *or* they do not believe it, but either way, they do not notice what the words are."[3]

Let's go back to Augustine. He advocated a beautiful intention for our engagement of Scripture: growth in love for God and neighbor. But there's a catch. To grow in love for God and neighbor, we must be willing to face the parts of ourselves that don't align with this intention. It's easy to see this lack in others, but it's painful to discover it inside ourselves.

To grow in love for God and neighbor, we must explore its opposite. The opposite of loving God for a believer is not hating God. It's indifference or apathy. Any cursory reading of the Bible will awaken us to difficulties that God's people had in remaining *faithful.* By indifference, I don't mean that we don't *care* about our relationship with God. It's more subtle. We tend to compartmentalize our lives. We have a space in our hearts that belongs fully to God, but there are plenty of rooms inside that belong to competing ideas. Yet anything that competes for our allegiance with God is a form of idolatry. So, to grow in love for Jesus we need to be willing to allow God through the Holy Spirit to probe our hearts with Scripture to show us areas where we do not truly *love* God.

The same is true for growth in love for our neighbor. The opposite of loving neighbor is not hatred; it's indifference. In

---

3   Alice Mary Hatfield, *Charles Williams: An Exploration of His Life and Works* (New York: Oxford University Press, 1983), 172.

this case, it's a lack of concern for others. It can rear its head in outright malice toward others. Most Christians don't openly desire evil for others. More often it is a subtle turning of our heads or closing our eyes to injustice.

Loving our neighbor involves a desire to do right for them. It's a commitment to concepts such as mercy, justice, reconciliation, and radical love. It's easy to love those who love us. But what of those who don't? Jesus tangibly extended love even to those who crucified him. What more powerful demonstration is there than Jesus' words on the Cross: "Father, forgive them; for they do not know what they are doing" (Luke 23:34). Moreover, Jesus always seemed to have the ability to see those in need around him. Scripture wants to stretch us by helping us to develop eyes to see those souls who are presently invisible to us. Are we willing to be challenged anew by the question that Jesus asked in the parable of the Good Samaritan: "Which . . . was a neighbor to the man?" (Luke 10:36).

To allow Scripture to do its work, we must hear the positive descriptions of love for God and neighbor in the texts we read. But we must also consent to allowing the Spirit to reveal to us areas where we don't truly love God and neighbor. This will involve learning to read the Bible anew and also, as we'll talk more about, *allowing the Bible to read us*. When new insights arise, we must have the courage to pray the ancient prayer: "Lord Jesus Christ, Son of God, have mercy on me, a sinner" and realign with the values of Jesus and his kingdom.

Are you ready to get started? Let me map out the journey that we'll take together in the rest of this book. First, in part 1, we'll explore models for understanding Scripture as revelation to us for living a life of love for God and neighbor. The goal is to describe how Scripture works in our lives and to begin to explore why we may struggle in reading it for deep spiritual formation.

In part 2, we'll confront head-on the issue of idolatry and the role of the unconscious in blocking the work of the Spirit in our lives. I'll introduce a method of reading that I've dubbed "idolatherapy." It's a form of divine therapy that directly targets the idolatry present in our lives. It's the interpretive lens that I've found helpful for opening my heart to God to the parts of my soul that hinder my growth in love. We'll explicitly explore how our brokenness, shame, biases, and sin seek to thwart God's work of deep personal and societal transformation.

In part 3, I'll model a way of reading that I believe honors Augustine's intention and hopefully serves you in your personal growth in love for God and neighbor. I'll share how to apply the principles from part 1 and part 2 in your own reading of Scripture by offering interpretations of selected passages in both the Old and New Testaments.

Questions for Reflection

- What do you think of Augustine's insistence that the goal of interpretation is learning how a text teaches us to better love God and neighbor?

- What do you think are your present blind spots when it comes to a deep reading of the Bible?

- What questions do you have so far?

Part One:
How Scripture Works in Our Lives

Chapter One:
Inspiration, Attention, and Astonishment

It is of the very nature of the Bible to affront,
perplex and astonish the human mind.

— Thomas Merton

Scripture is an essential means of grace that God uses to shape us into the people he created us to be. As Christians, we talk about the inspiration of Scripture. To speak of inspiration is to attempt to differentiate the words in the Bible from words in other books. Many writers and artists talk about being inspired. They likely were, in the sense that they worked out of an acknowledgment of serving something much bigger and grander than themselves. But Christians hold to an even larger view of inspiration. What is it that makes Scripture inspired in a way that is different from other works of art?

In 2 Timothy 3:16–4:2, Paul writes to his younger partner in ministry, Timothy:

All scripture is inspired by God and is useful for teaching, for reproof, for correction, and for training in righteousness, so that everyone who belongs to God may
be proficient, equipped for every good work. In the
presence of God and of Christ Jesus, who is to judge
the living and the dead, and in view of his appearing
and his kingdom, I solemnly urge you: proclaim the
message; be persistent whether the time is favorable or
unfavorable; convince, rebuke, and encourage, with
the utmost patience in teaching.

Paul's words are memorable because verse 16 contains
the claim that "all scripture is inspired by God." This text is
an obvious passage for establishing a doctrine of Scripture. It
reminds us that the words of Scripture are *God-breathed. God-
breathed* is the literal meaning of the Greek word translated
"inspired." To believe in the inspiration of Scripture is a core
element of the faith that has united Christians (and Jews with
respect to the Hebrew Scriptures) throughout history.

I'm not interested in attempting to defend the inspiration
of Scripture. I don't believe that Scripture requires defending.
It simply needs to be read. If we read the text, the Bible will do
its work. In fact, I truly believe that the greatest apologetic for
the Bible is its ability to describe the human condition ruthlessly
and point to the truth that God alone can redeem us from our
lostness, that God loves all souls enough to make redemption a
reality. Commit to reading the Bible faithfully, and I am confident that you will encounter the God who inspired the human
authors to write the Scriptural books. Even better, you will discover the God who created you and loves you unconditionally.

Yes, there are difficult texts in the Bible. Yes, parts of Scripture can seem outdated, irrelevant, or downright troubling. But as a person of faith, I approach Scripture with an openness and curiosity that we might describe as a posture of consent. Rather than being suspicious of what the Bible says, I choose to be interested and suspicious of my own reactions to what the Bible says. This is especially true of texts that directly challenge the way I presently live and the causes I currently serve. I fully consent to giving Scripture a reading even when I don't like what it says. For me, consent means this: I accept the Scriptures in their final form as the guide to helping us make our way through the world. I believe that the content of the Bible is as God intended it to be (including its messiness). My job as a reader is to open my heart and mind to it in order to understand its demands on my life and on the community of faith in which I live.

The attitude and curiosity that I bring to the act of reading the Bible set the limits on Scripture's ability to function as a means of grace. When I was young, I worked diligently to learn Greek, Hebrew, the historical background of the Bible times, and various interpretive methods. I wanted to master the Bible. As I've gotten older, I realize that all of this knowledge and skill is only helpful if I shift my goal to allowing the Bible to master me. This is the critical shift. Biblical authority is a way of life in which I willingly submit myself to the probing and investigation of the text. It is only then that the Bible truly functions as the Word of God for me and for my community.

Karl Barth distinguished between the Bible as the Word of God and the Bible becoming the Word of God. Barth's thinking is complex and nuanced. But at the core he makes a powerful observation. By distinguishing between the text as some sort of magical book (my words not Barth's) and the text as a vehicle for God's grace through the power of the Holy Spirit, the responsibility is put squarely on us as readers and hearers of the Word. Since the Bible *becomes* the Word of God through the Holy Spirit, we students must prepare ourselves for a conversation with it.

The Spirit enlivens the Word, but we can quench the Spirit's work in our lives. We can suppress the power of the Word consciously through inattentiveness, willful neglect, or rebellion. We can also negate its power unconsciously through blocks caused by our upbringing and our life experiences (both positive and negative ones).

John Steinbeck's *East of Eden* is a rich, modern retelling of the Cain and Abel story. One of my favorite parts is its description of the matriarch Liza Hamilton. She and her husband, Samuel, were immigrants from Ireland to the Salina Valley in California. Liza was depicted as the pious anchor of the family. She read the Bible regularly. Of her commitment to Scripture, Steinbeck wrote:

> Her total intellectual association was the Bible, except the talk of Samuel and her children, and to them she did not listen. In that one book she had her history and her poetry, her knowledge of peoples and things, her ethics, her morals, and her salvation. She never studied the Bible or inspected it; she just read it. The many places where it seems to refute itself did not confuse

her in the least. *And finally she came to a point where she knew it so well that she went right on reading it without listening.*[4]

I love that last line because it describes so well the temptation that many of us face when reading the Bible. It's clear that the Bible was an important part of her life, but she reached a point at which she stopped growing. She knew the Word, but she became unable to *hear* it, and thus it stopped shaping her life. The tragedy was that she didn't recognize this profound loss. She thought of the Bible as God's book, but it didn't function as the Word of God in her life because she stopped paying attention to it.

Wesley's comments in his *Notes* on the inspiration of Scripture described by Paul in 2 Timothy 3:16 are helpful: "The Spirit of God not only once inspired those who wrote it, but continually inspires, supernaturally assists, those that read it with earnest prayer."[5]

Wesley's words are helpful because he adds a human dimension to the role of reading Scripture. Don't pass over too quickly "those who read it with earnest prayer." We can avoid the danger of inattentiveness in our study of the Scripture by committing to reading it prayerfully. I'm not suggesting that every study session must involve an intentional practice such as *lectio divina*. I am, however, advocating that we pray for illumination, guidance, and astonishment before and during our

---

4   John Steinbeck, *East of Eden*, Steinbeck Centennial Edition (New York: Penguin, 2003), 43. Emphasis added.

5   John Wesley, *Wesley's Notes on the Bible*, 2 Timothy 3:16, accessed February 2, 2023, https://www.ccel.org/ccel/wesley/notes.i.xvii.iv.html.

wrestling with the Word. We want the Holy Spirit quickening our minds, imaginations, and hearts as we listen attentively to the text. To pray while studying reminds us that God has much more at stake in our interpretation than we do. Reading Scripture is about personal transformation for the purpose of societal transformation. Every reading of the text is always much bigger than our individual lives and agendas.

I've struggled at different times in my life to be truly attentive to the Bible. We all will likely experience seasons of spiritual dryness. During such times, it can feel as though we are merely going through the motions of reading God's Word. In these moments, it is critical to be self-aware of our spiritual condition. It is not time for self-flagellation. It is time to become genuinely curious about our reaction to the Word and to take Wesley's advice about praying earnestly.

"Lord, astonish me anew" is the prayer I like to use when I begin reading the Bible. I believe it is one of those prayer postures that God honors.

Also, I seek to be genuinely interested in finding what is lurking under my struggle to read Scripture attentively. Does some part of the text remind me of a pain point or struggle in my past or present? Does the text seem irrelevant to my current context, and if so, how do I wish the text would address my life or community? Do I sense a deep dissonance with the text, and if so, what would it look like for me to realign my head, heart, and hands with its message?

It's also possible to be inattentive due to the pressing needs of the day. Jesus warned about the distractions of life (even important matters, such as food and clothing) when he exhorted his followers, "But strive first for the kingdom of God and his righteousness, and all these things will be given to you as well" (Matt 6:33).

Part of a life shaped with Scripture involves learning to make time in the Word a "must" rather than a "should." We've all heard the sermon that in essence says, "You should read the Bible more." I don't care for the word "should." If you are reading this book, my goal is not to convince you that you *should* read the Bible. Instead, my desire is more audacious. In fact, I'll say this: I don't think you *should* read the Bible. "Shoulds" involve guilt, and the Gospel is about grace. I want to help you kindle or rekindle your love for how God can use Scripture for transformation to such a degree that reading Scripture becomes a "must" for you. I must read Scripture because I know that this practice is life-giving, soul-shaping, and transformational. To neglect it for any significant amount of time lessens my ability to grow in love for God, neighbor, and self.

Questions for Reflection

- What is your present understanding of the inspiration of the Bible?

- What role does curiosity play in your reading of the Bible and in your spiritual life in general?

- Describe a time when Scripture truly astonished you.

- Is reading Scripture a *should* or a *must*? What needs to shift in your life to make it a consistent *must*?

Chapter Two:
Our Conscious Neglect of Scripture

We can quench the Spirit's work in our lives through Scripture by conscious neglect. Conscious neglect is insidious because of the ease of sliding into this posture. Professional exegetes are particularly prone to it. What do I mean? Pastors and even biblical studies professors function as paid interpreters of the Scripture. Pondering the Bible is part of our job description. We preach sermons and teach Bible studies on a weekly basis. But it is easy to substitute the weekly work of reading Scripture for *others* for the daily practice of reading Scripture for the sake of our own souls. We focus on the need for finding a "message" to share rather than on our growth in grace and love. We forget our true identity as persons loved by God and instead live as purveyors of religious goods and services to others.

I am not questioning the motives of pastors and spiritual leaders. When I say "conscious," I'm not suggesting *intentionality*. No pastor or spiritual leader sets a goal of neglecting Scripture. It's something that slowly happens over time as we allow the pressing needs of ministry to constrict the spiritual formation that would truly allow us to flourish.

In his Sermon #18 on the Song of Songs, Bernard of Clairvaux uses the contrasting metaphors of a reservoir versus a canal to describe spiritual leaders. A pastor who ministers as a reservoir is deeply formed in God's grace. He or she has an abundance out of which to serve others. In Bernard's day, reservoirs were on hills. To minister as a reservoir is to dispense deep knowledge of God that comes out of the overflow as the waters pour over the top of the banks of the reservoir.

In contrast, some pastors minister as canals. In our day, a canal can be a permanent body of water that connects two major bodies of water. For example, the Panama Canal serves as a shortcut from the Pacific Ocean to the Caribbean. For Bernard, a canal was a dry waterway that only flowed after a storm. In urban areas, we'd call these "storm sewers." To minister as a canal means that whatever grace or blessing flows into us immediately flows back out of us. We are not growing but merely channeling our weekly knowledge to others.

As a seminarian, Lawson Stone, one my favorite professors, warned us to not worry about what we'd be preaching this coming Sunday. Instead, we needed to focus on the persons we'd be serving five, ten, and twenty years down the road. This was a powerful word for me. I needed to grow into a person deeply shaped by God for the long haul. Bernard was describing the same need. If we focus on the short term, that is, reading Scripture only for the next sermon, we slowly burn up all of our reserves. We become *canals*. Ironically, according to Bernard, we end up loving others *not as* we love ourselves, but we love others *more than* we love ourselves. Living this way is not sustainable for the life that God calls us to. Loving others more than you love yourself may sound noble, but it will slowly constrict your life. Too many of us burn out or lose our original passion for mission and ministry because we served others to the long-term neglect of our soul.

Choose today to cultivate a deep practice of intentional study of Scripture outside of your regular preparation for preaching and teaching. Such a practice will actually enliven your present teaching and preaching because you will be growing deeper roots yourself. You deserve deep roots. By the way, so do the people whom you are called to serve.

Before I conclude this chapter, let me add a final warning. We can also mute the work that God wants to do in our lives through willful disobedience. When we are struggling with Scripture, it is worth taking a hard look at ourselves:

Is there some part of me that no longer wants to grow in grace?

Is there some sin that I've been hiding from others?

Does my private backstage life not fully align with my onstage public life?

Am I harboring a spirit of unforgiveness toward someone?

Don't be afraid to answer these tough questions. Be honest and step back into the light of God's love and grace.

Questions for Reflection

- What do you presently do during "dry" seasons in your study of Scripture?

- What are your thoughts about Bernard's contrasting imagery of reservoir and canal? How would you assess your current life?

Chapter Three:
Inspiration, Human and Divine

In the next few chapters, I want to explore various facets of what the divine inspiration of Scripture means and the human role in recording and interpreting God's words. We'll begin by addressing the reality that the Bible was written by persons just like us. Scripture is 100 percent the product of fully human authors and editors working over the centuries. The process of recognizing certain books as holy Scripture was also 100 percent the product of the deliberation and discernment of faith communities. Before I lose you, let me explain why the full recognition of the human nature of the Bible is important. The Bible is not a magical book. Its authors were writing to people in their day to exhort and encourage them to live faithfully in relationship to God. This was true of both the Old Testament and New Testament books. They wrote the original texts in Hebrew and Aramaic for the Old Testament and in Greek for the New Testament. They used the language, style, and thought forms of their day to describe what they believed God to be inspiring them to write.

Yes, I still believe in the full divine inspiration of the text despite the previous paragraph. In fact, I believe that Scripture is 100 percent the product of the work of the Holy Spirit. This includes the inspiration of the authors and editors. I also believe that the Spirit was at work in the communities that first received the biblical books and guided God's people to recognize over time the authority of these documents above all others for the purpose of right belief and faithful living. Moreover, I fully recognize that the Spirit remains active today to help us receive, read, and interpret the life-giving good news of the Bible today.

So how do we sort out the human from the divine in Scripture? I'd suggest that we don't have to. My first Old Testament teacher Lawson Stone, whom I mentioned in the previous chapter, shared a Christological model for understanding Scripture. He argued as I have above that the Bible is 100 percent human and 100 percent divine in a way analogous to how we think about the natures of Jesus.[6] Jesus was and is fully human while simultaneously being fully divine. Yes, this is one of the mysteries of faith, but that's ok. We can approach the Bible with a "faith seeking understanding" posture in which we recognize the need to study and address the human aspects of Scripture without denying that these texts contain the Word of God for us. In other words, to talk about the divine inspiration of the

---

6   The "hypostatic union" explains the union of both human and divine in one person. Jesus is simultaneously both 100 percent human and 100 percent divine. This was affirmed by the Athanasian Creed, composed most likely in the fifth century.

Bible does not force us into suppressing the human dimension of Scripture. Nor does recognizing the historical rootedness of Scripture in the life of ancient faith communities and cultures mute the power of these documents to speak deep truth to us today. It is incorrect to imagine the human and divine aspects of Scripture as if we are talking about a pizza. If there are five slices that we assign to human production, then that leaves three pieces for the divinity. Our analogy instead is that there are actually two entire pizzas in one: 100 percent human pizza and 100 percent divine pizza.

I appreciate the way N. T. Wright describes the relationship between faith in the divine and a recognition of the human historical processes at work. Much of Wright's work has focused on understanding the historical Jesus. In his popular book cowritten with Marcus Borg, *The Meaning of Jesus*, Wright describes a "faith divorced from history" as being indicative of one imprisoned in the attic of one's house whereas "history divorced from faith" is an equally problematic bondage in the basement. Writing about his historical research on Jesus, he can write, "The more I find out about Jesus historically, the more I find that my faith-knowledge of him is supported and filled out."[7] To make this more specifically related to our topic, I think we can easily rewrite this statement to read, "The more I find out about Scripture historically, that is, the human dimensions, the more I find my faith-knowledge about it supported and filled out."

---

7   Marcus J. Borg and N. T. Wright, *The Meaning of Jesus : Two Visions* (San Francisco: HarperOne, 2007), 26.

Allow me one more extended quote from Wright on this topic:

> History, then, prevents faith from becoming fantasy. Faith prevents history becoming mere antiquarianism. Historical research, being always provisional, cannot ultimately veto faith, though it can pose hard questions of that faith, in order to retain its integrity precisely as *Christian* faith it must struggle to answer, and may well grow strong through answering. Faith, being subject to the vagaries of personality and culture, cannot veto the historical enterprise (it can't simply say, "I don't like the Jesus you write about, so you must be wrong"), but it can put hard questions to history, not least on the large topic of the origins of Christianity, and history may be all the better for trying to answer them.[8]

Questions for Reflection

- What does it mean that Scripture is 100 percent divine and 100 percent human?

- What is your current understanding of the relationship between faith and history?

---

8   Borg and Wright, 26–27.

Chapter Four:
The Wesleyan Quadrilateral and Our Blind Spots

Reading Scripture involves the interplay between our personal experience, traditional understandings about the Bible over the course of church history, and reason. Of course, we are talking about the human side of interpretation. In this chapter, I want to explore a model to help make sense of what takes place when we seek to hear from God in our reading of the Bible.

Methodist scholar Albert Outler famously coined the expression the "Wesleyan Quadrilateral" to explain what information we use to form our beliefs and practices of faith. Outler was attempting to summarize the dynamic relationship between Scripture, reason, tradition, and experience in theological reflection on faith and practice. The danger (which Outler never intended) was that, for some, this elevated human experience, Christian tradition, and reason to equal status with the Bible. Many have stopped using the term "Wesleyan Quadrilateral" because of problematic misuses of it. But I think that it remains a useful model for thinking about how Scripture shapes us.

My former colleague Paul Chilcote brilliantly suggests that we think of Scripture, reason, tradition, and experience as parts of a wind chime.[9] First, every wind chime has a base that serves as the anchor for the rest of the chime. Scripture is the base. Without the base there is no wind chime. Without Scripture, there can be no authentic theological reflection. But a wind chime cannot sound out its notes without the actual chimes. In this case, tradition, reason, and experience serve as the chimes. All three are attached directly to the base. This establishes the critical link between reason, tradition, experience, and Scripture. It emphasizes the authoritative role that the Bible plays in theological, ethical, and spiritual reflection. It is the primary source for our faith and practice.

Scripture sings, if you will, through the chimes of experience, reason, and tradition. But the chimes will make no sound without the ball or hammer that hangs from the center of the base. The Christian community (readers of the text) represent the ball or hammer of the wind chime. It is the readers of the text who make it sing through reason, tradition, and experience. Readers must take up the text and listen attentively to it.

Yet even with all of these elements a wind chime is mute unless the actual wind blows and creates the clanging of the chimes against the ball or hammer. Of course, it is the Holy Spirit who represents the wind that makes Scripture sing its

---

9   Paul W. Chilcote, "Rethinking the Wesleyan Quadrilateral," in *The Quest for Love Divine: Select Essays in Wesleyan Theology and Practice* (Eugene, OR: Cascade Books, 2022), 81–83.

beautiful song for the believing community through reason, tradition, and experience.

This model is powerful because it takes into account the full complexity of what it actually means to read and receive a true word from God and respects the critical role that human experience plays in our reading of Scripture. Truth must be embodied. Scripture is not just for our minds; it is for our hands and heart as well. A life formed by Scripture is one in which we can *see*, *touch*, and *hear* the fruits of the Spirit in a person's life.

Recognizing the role of experience sometimes receives undue criticism. But experience recognizes that we readers have actual "skin in the game." We are looking not merely to understand Scripture's message but to live it out authentically. At least two blind spots exist involving the use of personal experience.

The first blind spot involves emphasizing the full authority of Scripture and its message. We may understand the *what* of Scripture, that is, what it meant or its theological implications, but we then fail to press on to the *how*. By *how*, my assumption is that Scripture is meant to be lived out moment by moment. Understanding the meaning of a text in my experience does not necessarily translate to a transformed life. One of the things that I appreciate about the legacy of Wesley was his emphasis on living out the Word. He is often dismissed as a "practical theologian." But his genius in part involved "teaching plain truth to plain people." He broke down the text and key doctrines to show his Methodist followers not merely *what* to believe but *how* to live out their beliefs. He taught an *experiential* faith that pointed to holiness of heart and life in *this* present life.

The second blind spot relates to the first but is its opposite. If the first blind spot risks overemphasizing the *what* of the meaning of the text over the *how* of living it out, the second blind spot risks declaring that the *how* of living is defined more by our personal experience than by the plain meaning of the text. As I've suggested already, our commitment to Scripture is most evident when its message challenges our present belief structure and ethic *and* we reassess our lived experience in light of Scripture. Yes, our experiences must be taken seriously. Our experiences will often ask hard questions of the text and challenge previous readings. But when our lives do not line up with what we discern the biblical text to be teaching, we must not mute the text. Sometimes we simply need to open up our lives to the deep questions and invitation to growth that the Bible is presenting.

The Quadrilateral also understands the rootedness of faith in the two-thousand-year tradition of the Church. What Scripture means today has continuity with what it's meant to previous generations. This isn't to say that we can't receive a new word, but tradition serves a critical role in hearing the Scripture. Part of wrestling with the meaning of a biblical text involves grappling with how other readers of the Bible have understood and applied the text in the past. If we read the text in isolation, we lose the wisdom of the Church through the ages. I often tell my students that they may indeed discover a unique reading of the Bible through personal study, but then I offer a warning. If our reading of the text does not stand in some continuity with previous readings, we may be *misreading* the text. By saying this, I am not suggesting that biblical interpretation involves inhabiting a silo or echo chamber cut off from the world. In fact, *misreadings* often arise out of echo chambers. We need to seek out not merely past readings that agree with us but especially readings that stand in opposition or at least offer nuances to our readings. We must make certain that we study the best of the past.

Last, the Quadrilateral respects the role of human reason. We can bring our best thinking and giftedness to reading the Bible. We don't have to be naive or superstitious in our engagement of the text. The Bible isn't a magical book. We employ no "secret" interpretive strategies that unveil hidden mysteries. Scripture's human authors wrote in the living languages of their day employing the rhetoric, artistry, and creativity that all writing involves. Scripture's writers were products of their ancient times and worldviews as well. To say this does not make their writing antiquated, nor does it mean that they were unable to rise above their historical situation to speak of the future. I want merely to state the obvious: to read Scripture wisely and well involves us bringing our best intellectual rigor to the task. Again, reflection is a two-way conversation. I cannot set myself up as superior to the biblical author merely because I live in the nuclear age and have a radically different worldview regarding science. Part of employing reason involves our commitment to learn about the ancient context and its thought forms in order to read the text in light of its historical background. But I cannot stop there. To use my mind also involves bringing difficult questions from the modern world to bear on the text.

My favorite part of Chilcote's wind chime illustration is his recognition that *wind* must be present for the wind chime to sing its song. Scripture remains a product of the ancient world *unless* the Spirit enlivens it anew in our day. I think we sometimes forget this. It doesn't require a PhD in biblical studies to read the Bible in powerful ways. A faithful believer with a limited education is fully capable of receiving and proclaiming a powerful interpretation. In fact, through the ages, we see examples of illiterate preachers and teachers who on memory alone have taught the Scriptures.

Of course, methodology and training matter. But it is the Spirit's work (and not ours) to convict another's heart and create true transformation.

Every pastor at some point will have this experience: We've just preached our hearts out. As we greet folks at the door, an excited listener stops to share with us what he or she gained from the message. This person has obviously been deeply touched, but after sharing the testimony of the Word that person received, we have to hide the confusion that we feel, because we know that we did not say any of the things that this person "heard" in the sermon.

Other times we prayerfully craft a message. We've done careful exegesis. We found clear and relevant language and illustrations to share the biblical truth. We delivered the message to the best of our ability. It seemed to flow well, and we feel in the zone. We sensed God's presence in the service. But there appeared to be zero response from our hearers that day.

The parable of the soils (Matt 13:1–23) is critical in understanding these dynamics. As readers of the Word, our job is twofold: (1) we need to assess our hearts so that we are open to growth, and (2) we need to *sow* persistently in the full knowledge that not all of the soil will bear full fruit. In 1 Corinthians 3:5–10, Paul reminds us that it is God who brings growth. How does God do this? It's through the Spirit. The Spirit makes the Scriptures sing to those who have ears to hear!

Don't ever forget that the Holy Spirit is fully capable of surprising us with the Word. God has more invested in our work with the text than we do. Bring all of yourself to the text and let all of the text speak to you and your audience.

Questions for Reflection

- What is your impression of the Wesleyan Quadrilateral?
- What is the role of the Holy Spirit in the reading of the Word?

Chapter Five:
The Transcendence of God and Why It Matters for Understanding the Bible

God is knowable. Yet God is greater than we are capable of comprehending and imagining. The dilemma that we face as budding theologians and interpreters of Scripture is to bridge the tension between knowledge of God and the mystery of God.

Let's be clear. To say that God is knowable involves *faith*. It's a matter of trust. More specifically, it involves answering this question: Whom or what do I trust to provide me with clear and authoritative instruction about God to guide me through life?

I'm always mindful of the iconic story in Genesis 3 where Eve and the serpent speak. The serpent begins with a well-formed question: "Did God really say . . . ?" (Gen 3:1 NIV). The serpent in essence questions God's trustworthiness. But this conversation is even more powerful when we think of it in terms of *revelation* and *knowledge*. How do we know what God said? Dietrich Bonhoeffer remarks that this dialogue was the "first conversation about God."[10] When we read the narratives at the beginning of the book of Genesis, Genesis 3 marks a watershed moment. It is the point at which God moves from *subject* to *object*. Up to that point, God and humanity interacted freely. God has personally instructed Adam about the garden and the available and abundant food for their consumption (2:9, 16). God had also clearly established the tree of the knowledge of good and evil as off-limits (2:17).

In the conversation that leads to Adam and Eve consuming the forbidden fruit, they speak of God in the third person. We also speak *about* God. We do it so often today that we rarely recognize this reality. Next time you are at church, ponder how much talk occurs *about* God rather than actual conversation *with* God. We can easily do this in our reading of Scripture as well. Our interpretive work can become a conversation with ourself, other believers, or even commentators about the meaning of the passage.

The danger is this: we can substitute our experiences, church tradition, human reason, our favorite ideology, our politics, our hermeneutic, our view of the world, or our culture for the Word of God revealed in the Scriptures.

In the Genesis 3 scene, we often focus on the role of the serpent. Church tradition has identified the serpent as Satan. Often when we think of Satan, we think of a powerful evil

---

10   Dietrich Bonhoeffer, *Creation and Fall: A Theological Exposition of Genesis 1–3* (Minneapolis: Fortress, 2004), 111.

force, and we imagine Eve and Adam as helpless in his presence. Yet the text narrates a conversation rather than a display of Satan's power. Adam and Eve do resort to a "the devil made me do it" defense (v. 13.), but this is more excuse making than reality. The serpent merely uses questions and observations; he does not use any supernatural powers.

The issue is fundamentally one of trust. The serpent suggests that God is not trustworthy. Adam and Eve would be better served not believing God's instructions. Perhaps the creator's prohibition against eating from the tree of the knowledge of good and evil is a selfish one rather than a life-giving one. Perhaps God does not in fact have their best interests at heart.

For me *trust* is the issue in approaching Scripture. Is the Bible what it claims to be or not? Can I trust that the infinite God has indeed inspired and preserved in human language a text that serves as an authoritative guide to life? Do I indeed trust that if I live my life in light of Scripture, I am choosing my own ultimate good as well as modeling a mode of life that is good for others and for the world?

What happens when I lose trust in God's Word? I'm left floundering. Let's go back to the Genesis 3 story. What happens when Eve and Adam lose their faith in God's trustworthiness? They do what each of us does. They trust themselves to make their way through the world. If Scripture is not trustworthy, we are left to our own devices. In such cases, we will elevate experience, reason, tradition, and the voices of our friends above the message of the text.

I fully recognize the complexity of understanding certain biblical texts. I am not advocating a "God said it, I believe it, that settles it" fundamentalism that denies the presence of uncertainty. Interpretation is hard work. But what I am saying is this: we must be self-aware and honest in our reading of the Bible. If a text is clear and it challenges our current mode of living, we must realign with the text. Our willingness to change in light of the text's critique is how we demonstrate our trust.

So, back to the tension between God as knowable and God as greater than we are capable of understanding and comprehending. Most of us don't enjoy the experience of this tension. We'd rather resolve tensions by gravitating to one side or the other. Our modern world amplifies this reality, and the various polarizations (red/blue, progressive/traditionalist, etc.) are the result.

The problem with binary thinking is that God is in the poles while simultaneously being beyond them. In theological terms, God is both transcendent and immanent. We'll explore both of these terms in our discussion.

When we speak of God as transcendent, we are recognizing God's "otherness." God is the Creator and stands outside of time, space, and reality. God is not the universe. God is the creator of the universe in all of its complexity and depth. Imagine that we can draw a circle around all that the universe entails, including the idea of infinity. Outside of that circle is the God of the Bible. God is holy. God is the standard bearer for truth, and God is wholly other as the only Being that has no beginning or end.

As twenty-first century humans, we stand in awe of the immensity and complexity of the universe around us. Theoretical physics speculates and ponders mind-expanding ideas such as parallel universes, worm holes, and time travel. To reflect on God as the architect of our seemingly infinitely complex universe boggles the mind. It makes us rightfully feel small. Heck, I feel small every time I'm out in nature, let alone pondering my finiteness in the face of the limited amount we know about the world. How could we ever *know* the creator if we struggle to make sense of our own inner complexity, let alone the vastness of creation? How could the Bible—a collection of books from the Iron, Hellenistic, and Roman ages—offer a compelling guide to know this God or how to live in the modern world? If God exists, how could the Bible be anything more than one guide among many to truth?

Scripture also affirms that God is immanent. For God to be immanent means that God is fully present and active in our world. God is with us. There isn't any part of the world in which God lacks presence. Unlike transcendence, which emphasizes the "otherness of God," immanence points to the knowability of God. God is near; therefore, we can know God.

The challenge of immanence is this: if God is everywhere, then perhaps God is nowhere. What do I mean by this? The danger of *immanence* lies in making God indistinct from creation. God becomes the warmth of the sun or the laws of nature or our personal experiences. The problem of immanence is that the natural world and our experiences support a variety of interpretations–some of which are contradictory. Does creation point to a good God or an evil God? If merely observing the world leads to the recognition of the wide diversity of human experiences, how does one assert the universality and authority of any ethical system over others?

It seems to me that both poles can lead us to the same place. They solve the inherent problems by imagining God in our own image. If God is radically transcendent, then revelation is unavailable or impossible to understand. Therefore, we make our way through the world with the resources available to us—our strengths, knowledge, experience, reason, and lessons from our community. Scripture may still be read, but it is only one witness among others, because it is primarily a human book that shares the past religious experiences of our predecessors. It is inspired but only as a human witness that exists, as one inspired work among many. In other words, Scripture is no longer *uniquely* inspired in a way that is qualitatively distinct from other products of human inspiration.

If God is immanent apart from being transcendent, we may also turn to our experiences as the final arbiter. Without transcendence to set absolute and timeless standards, everything becomes fluid and subject to the various contexts and cultures of the world. Whatever *is true* for a community becomes the norm or standard. Again, the Bible may be read and may even be understood conceptually as God's Word, but it is fundamentally our personal lenses that give meaning to the Bible. The same passage of Scripture may then mean one thing to, say, a white male evangelical of European descent who is living in a rural part of the United States, and something radically different to, say, a Latina Pentecostal dwelling in a barrio in Ecuador or a young Anglican mother in Nigeria.

Also, apart from transcendence, a fully immanent God can easily disappear into an indistinct spirituality formed by human experience. We functionally create God in our image. Scripture becomes an illustration for the ideas and thoughts that we bring from our culture, upbringing, and experiences to the text. The Bible functions as a mirror that merely reflects who we already are. The tragedy of modern life is our tendency to equate loving others with an unconditional acceptance of even actions that may bring harm to self or others. Scripture wants more for us. It teaches us deep truths of God's love for us, but it never loses site of the larger goal. God loves us so much that he wants to guide us into deeper and deeper levels of growth in grace and love. In other words, God's love always invites us to even deeper levels of transformation. Who we are today pales in comparison to who we are becoming through the purifying love of God. This is true for the most ripened saint or the most obstinate sinner, as growth in God's love is an infinite game.

The Bible holds together the tension between God as unknowable and God as fully knowable. It does this by affirming transcendence and immanence simultaneously. Listen to a few of my favorite texts from the Old Testament. In Isaiah 6, the prophet testifies to his experience of encountering the Lord in the temple. As part of this powerful encounter, Isaiah hears two heavenly beings proclaim these words (v. 3):

Holy, holy, holy is the lord of hosts;
the whole earth is full of his glory.

Transcendence and immanence are on full display here. In the first line, the threefold repetition of holy is a bold declaration that the Lord is the holiest of all. In other words, the God whom Isaiah experiences is radically separate and distinct from creation. God is not part of creation. God stands outside of time and space. This is transcendence in full view. Moreover, the idea of holy as an attribute of God carries a moral element as well. As the holiest of all, God is the standard of ethical uprightness. God does the right thing, at the right time, every time. God is undivided in his intentions and actions.

The second line captures God's immanence. Yes, God is holy and transcendent, but creation is the platform for displaying God's glory or awesomeness. The Holy One fills creation with his renown and weightiness. Yet how is the Holy One known? God calls and sends Isaiah to speak in human language to God's people. God's words interpret in human language the meaning of God's presence in the world.

Psalm 113 is another text that simultaneously illustrates transcendence and immanence. This is a hymn of praise for who God is and what God does. Who is God? Observe how verses 4–6 describe his incomparability:

The Lord is high above all nations,

and his glory above the heavens.

Who is like the Lord our God,

who is seated on high,

Who looks far down

on the heavens and the earth.

This is transcendence. Psalm 113 imagines God residing in a space where God has to look far down not merely on the earth but even on the heavens.

Yet the transcendent God is immanent. Verses 7–9 describe the meaning of God's nearness to us:

> He raises the poor from the dust,
>
> and lifts the needy from the ash heap,
>
> to make them sit with princes,
>
> with the princes of his people.
>
> He gives the barren woman a home,
>
> making her the joyous mother of children.
>
> Praise the Lord!

The contrast between these two parts of the psalm is telling. God is so transcendent that God looks down on the heavens. Yet this same God is immanent to such a degree that God pays attention to the exploited, marginalized, and outcasts of society. God demonstrates his character by reversing the fortune of those on the bottom of human hierarchies. God's immanence isn't one that merely rubber-stamps human experience. God's immanence transforms human experience. It is not a scenario in which the powerful and well-connected simply gain even greater levels of influence and wealth. The biblical witness imagines a world in which by the power of God the weak become strong, the poor become rich, and the childless become parents. It would be a profound misstep to read such statements as revolutionary ones in which the 1 percent are cut down to size. Yes, God is fully capable of judgment, but Psalm 113 captures true abundance. The psalmist doesn't merely imagine God taking from the top and giving it to the bottom in a way that merely *redistributes injustice*. In God's economy, princes remain princes, but the poor and needy become royalty as well. We become true equals as members of the body of Christ.

By the way, I am not denying the reality of God's wrath and the human desire for vengeance. We'll address it in chapter 17 of this book when we tackle head-on one of the most difficult prayers in the Bible (Psalm 137:9): "Happy shall they be who take your little ones and dash them against the rock!"

The most sublime connection of God as knowable and God as unknowable is Jesus Christ. Jesus is God incarnate. As the creeds affirm, Jesus is fully human and fully divine. Jesus is the Word made flesh (John 1:14). Jesus "is the image of the invisible God, the first born of all creation" (Col 1:15). Jesus "was in the form of God" (Phil 2:6) but self-emptied and died a death reserved for a slave (2:7–8). Jesus became a human male approximately two thousand years ago; yet the Son is eternal and present and participated in the creation of the world.

Jesus shows us God in profound ways. We know from Moses' experiences that God cannot be seen face-to-face, yet when we see Jesus, we see God. John puts it this way: "No one has ever seen God. It is God the only Son, who is close to the Father's heart, who has made him known" (John 1:18).

God is transcendent *and* immanent. God is knowable because God has made God's self known through Jesus Christ.

But what we ultimately know about Jesus Christ is transmitted through the Bible. Thus, the Bible is the means by which God mediates to humanity the good news of the Gospel. We do not have to claim that we know everything about God. This is heresy. God is greater than any thought that we can ever conceive. We will always have mystery. To recognize our finiteness and inability to grasp and understand the totality of God, however, does not mean that we know *nothing* or that we must reduce God to some *mirroring* of a part of creation or some human ideology.

Instead, we recognize in Scripture the means of learning *enough* about reality, ourselves, and God to journey through this world. Perhaps John Wesley captured it best in this well-known passage from his preface to the collection of his sermons:

"I want to know one thing, the way to heaven; how to land safe on that happy shore. God himself has condescended to teach the way; for this very end he came from heaven. He hath written it down in a book! O, give me that book! At any price, give me the Book of God! I have it: here is knowledge enough for me. Let me be [a man of one book]." [11] [12]

Whatever else Scripture is, we must approach it as an authoritative witness to guide us to life in the coming age. Wesley's posture is the right one.

---

11 Wesley used the Latin *homo unius libri*, which means "person of one book."

12 John Wesley, *The Works of the Reverend John Wesley,* vol. 5 (New York: J. & J. Harper, 1830), 4.

Questions for Reflection

- What does God's transcendence mean for you, and what role does it play in your reading of Scripture?

- What does immanence mean for you, and what role does it play in your reading of Scripture?

- What do you think Wesley meant by his desire to be a "man of one book"?

Chapter Six:
Psalm 19—the Witness of Creation and "God Who Speaks"

Psalm 19 is a sublime witness to the power of Scripture for witnessing to God and for transforming our lives. Of Psalm 19, C. S. Lewis wrote, "I take this to be the greatest poem in the Psalter and one of the greatest lyrics in the world."[13] Part of the artistry of Psalm 19 is found in its movement from the heavens declaring God's glory in verse 1 to the psalmist joining the chorus of creation by adding his or her voice in praising the Lord in the closing verse (14). Psalm 19 solves the tension between God as unknowable and God as knowable by naming the Torah as the key mediator of *knowledge* about the transcendent creator. But it is not mere *knowledge*. It is *saving* knowledge. By this I mean it is a knowledge that *transforms* us when we grasp it.

Psalm 19 divides into two sections: verses 1–6 and verses 7–14. In verses 1–6, the focus is on creation as a witness. Verse

---

13 C. S. Lewis, *Reflections on the Psalms* (New York: HarperOne, 1958), 73.

1 memorably asserts that "the heavens are telling the glory of God; and the firmament proclaims his handiwork."

English readers miss the subtlety found in the original Hebrew of verse 1. The word translated "God" is *El.* The problem we have as English readers is that we are unable to recognize that *El* is not the typical word used for "God" in the Old Testament. The most common word translated "God" is *Elohim.* For example, Genesis 1:1 reads "*Elohim* created the heavens and the earth.

Why does this matter? *El* is a generic way of referring to God in the Old Testament. *El* was also the proper name of the Canaanite god of creation. I'm not suggesting that Psalm 19 was a hymn of praise to the Canaanite god, but I am suggesting that the use of *El* is significant in relationship to what verse 1 is saying. The use of *El* in verse 1 also stands in contrast to the sevenfold recurrence of *Yahweh* ("Lord") in verses 7–14. *Yahweh* is the proper name of the God of the Old Testament. Yahweh is the name revealed to Moses at Sinai (see Exodus 3 and 6). Yahweh is the God who brought Israel out of Egypt (Exod 20:2). Yahweh self-defines as "a God merciful and gracious, slow to anger, and abounding in steadfast love and faithfulness, keeping steadfast love for the thousandth generation, forgiving iniquity and transgression and sin" (Exod 34:6–7a).

What is going on here? Why does the psalmist use *El* one time in verses. 1–6 and then *Yahweh* seven times in verses. 7–14?

Verses 1–6 point to what theologians call *general revelation. General revelation* refers to the clues that God has made available *widely* to all creatures and people. It is what we may infer or know about God by observing the created world. Such evidence is often disputed matter. Some see evidence of an intelligent design and thus full of purpose; others see the universe as the product of chance and devoid of meaning.

Nature is often breathtaking. In my limited experiences, I've seen the majestic mountains of the Rockies. I've marveled at the height of the waterfalls in El Yunque in Puerto Rico. I've felt the force of a category 4 hurricane shaking my house to its foundation and tearing apart my roof. I've attempted to surf ten-feet-tall waves and felt their crushing power when I wiped out.

Most of us can agree that nature makes us feel small and insignificant. Some might even say that creation is glorious. To speak of glory brings us back to Psalm 19. Verse 1a reads, "The heavens are telling the glory of God [El]." *Glory* at its core means "heaviness" or "weightiness." "Awesomeness" is also a possible translation. That feeling of smallness in the presence of something beyond us or greater than us is a natural response to an experience of *glory*.

Nature is revelatory in the sense of its ability both to astound and confound us with its complexity, beauty, randomness, expansiveness, and chaos-inducing violence. Creation demonstrates its own awesomeness. But the issue turns on this question: What is the effect of nature's revelation? Is the revelation from observing creation enough to bring us to a saving faith?

These questions lead us back to Psalm 19 and the psalmist's decision to use the generic "el" instead of "Yahweh" (Lord). Psalm 19:1 declares that there is a revelation of "God's" glory, but the next verses immediately deconstruct this claim. Verses 1–2 and 4a talk about the creation as though it speaks *clearly* about God. Yet verse 3 asserts the opposite: "There is no speech, nor are there words; their voice is not heard." What is going on here? Does creation speak about "God" or not?

The key is to recognize the use of "El" instead of "Elohim" or "Yahweh." To say the word "god" in the ancient world begged the question, "To which deity are you referring?" In the ancient world, there were hundreds if not thousands of different gods and goddesses. Most ancient peoples had creation myths and recognized a particular god or goddess as being somewhat in control of the process that brought forth the world as we know it. I use the term "somewhat" because in ancient paganism there was never a monotheistic claim that one deity created all that exists.

Let's return to the twenty-first century and ponder what this has to do with reading Scripture or understanding our world today. Most of my readers are likely living in the United States or at least some part of the English-speaking world. A Judeo-Christian worldview has been foundational for understanding reality until recently. Part of this worldview has been a monotheistic belief in one God to the exclusion of the claims of other religions.

Yet as I write these words in 2023, the meaning of the word "god" is now a contested one. I often hear in casual conversation exhortations such as this: "Pray to God or the universe or whatever higher power in which you believe." There are best-selling books such as *The Universe Has Your Back*. Most of us have friends, neighbors, or coworkers who practice religions other than Christianity or Judaism. Our world is no less spiritual than before, but our conception of God has become more ambiguous. God can be an energy field, creation itself, or even how we view our true self. For a materialist or atheist, the word *God* can even become a placeholder for unexplained parts of the universe.

All of this is a long way of affirming both Psalm 19's insistence and its denial of the power of creation to communicate truth. Yes, creation serves as a potent witness to *glory* in the sense that it makes us *feel small*, but does it teach us enough to change us or save us from the deepest problems that we face as humans?

The biblical claim is that there is only one God who can save us. This God is the one who stands beyond and above creation—the sole creator of the world, Yahweh. Beginning in verse 7, the psalmist introduces us to the only sure source of saving truth and knowledge: the *Torah* of Yahweh.

The core idea of Psalm 19 is critical for our thinking about Scripture. Psalm 19 is profoundly confident of God's presence and nature's ability to awaken us to something, or more correctly someone, bigger than we are. Glory is present in creation. But here is the challenge: How can we know this God? How do we live in light of God's glory?

The witness of Psalm 19 is the good news that God has spoken through the Torah of Yahweh. In fact, it is the Torah that reveals the character and nature of the God of whom creation speaks. In contrast to the verses 1–6, there is no ambiguity over the identity of God. The God of whom the heavens speak

is named Yahweh. Yahweh—or Lord, in English translations—
is named seven times in verses 7–14. Seven is a number that
points to completeness in the Bible. Think of the seven days of
creation in Genesis 1 or the seven churches in Revelation 2–3.

In verses 7–9, there is a sixfold repetition of Yahweh used
in a recurring structure that paints a portrait of Torah and its
transformational effect on those who engage it.

This recurring structure in verses 7–9 includes (1) a syn-
onym for *Torah* followed by (2) an adjective and then (3) a
phrase describing the resulting transformation:

> the law of the Lord is perfect, reviving the soul;
>
> the decrees of the Lord are sure, making wise the simple;
>
> the precepts of the Lord are right, rejoicing the heart;
>
> the commandment of the Lord is clear, enlightening
> the eyes;
>
> the fear of the Lord is pure, enduring forever;
>
> the ordinances of the Lord are true and righteous
> altogether.

The expanded vocabulary for Torah is important to observe:
Torah (law), decrees, precepts, commandment, fear, and ordi-
nances. Unlike the witness of creation in verses 1–6, there is no
ambiguity. Torah is an objective reality that can be heard, seen,
and even felt. By "felt," I'm referring to the outlier in the six
words: fear. All of the others point to an *objective* reality, that is
Israel's Scripture, but fear is a *subjective* response. It is not fear
for fear's sake. It is fear of the Lord. In the context of Psalm 19,

this is a fear or reverence in response to the *revelation of Yahweh*. It is not merely a fear induced by the feeling of smallness one experiences as a creature in the vast universe in which we live.

Unlike the revelation of nature, Torah creates its own response. An encounter with the Torah of Yahweh transforms its hearer. It is effectual. The assumption of the psalm is that the audience is receptive and open. Psalm 19 is not articulating a theology of the Word of God in which Scripture is a book of spells that manipulate a reader or hearer against his or her will. But Psalm 19 clearly declares the effectual power of Torah to do its work in a reader or hearer who desires to *know* the living God and is *willing* to open his or her heart to Scripture's message.

Psalm 19 along with Psalms 1 and 119 serve as Torah psalms. One of the key implications of these three Psalms was the elevation to the Psalter itself to *authoritative teaching* but also the Prophets and the Writings.[14] They are part of the movement within ancient Israel to a Torah-based piety. The faithful in ancient Israel found in the Torah, the Prophets, and the Writings the Word of God. The truth about God was mediated through inspired books. The key however is to recognize that this truth is transformational. It does not leave its hearer unchanged.

For the author of Psalm 19, the power of Torah to change a life is on full display. Verses 11–13 cut to the chase. Studying the authoritative instruction of God mediated through the Scriptures is the means to deep transformation. The goal is a wholeness that makes us aware of our "errors" and "hidden

---

14   James L. Mays, *The Lord Reigns: A Theological Handbook to the Psalms* (Louisville: Westminster John Knox, 1994), 128–35.

faults." Most of us recognize the blatant sins in our lives. How many of us are open to the sins that emerge from the deep swamplands inside of us? Yet the Psalmist recognizes in the Torah of the Lord a tool that God has gifted the faithful to promote a deep cleansing that can lead us to profound levels of conversion. Listen to the hopeful nature of verse 13b: "Then I shall be blameless, and innocent of great transgression."

Why do we need deep cleansing? It's not merely for our sake. Too often our spirituality is mere navel-gazing. Spirituality can become solely about our growth and experience. At worse this means: I want more of God so that I personally can find eternal security and inner peace. Of course, I'd prefer heaven over hell too. But the Psalmist has a bigger vision for life than a self-focused spirituality. The psalmist understands the stakes. The psalmist recognizes the importance of each human person. The good news of transformation is a message that must be shared.

The declarations of the heavens are all well and good, but they are not clear enough to effect the change that our world needs. Verses 1–6 make this clear. No one *knows* the truth about Yahweh by merely observing creation. Creation points to the reality of something bigger than us, but the specifics of this reality are ambiguous.

Yet the world needs clarity about Yahweh. God's mission to a lost, broken, and divided humanity depends on the spread of *clear* and *compelling* revelation. God's people have received such news through Scripture. Verses 11–13 reflect on what happens if and when we come to Scripture hungry and ready for transformation. The end result of Scripture's ability to transform us is *mission*.

The concluding verse of Psalm 19 is perhaps even more well-known than its opening verses. Many pastors and teachers use verse 14 as a prayer before speaking: "Let the words of my mouth and the meditation of my heart be acceptable to you, O lord, my rock and my redeemer."

Verse 14 is the true climax of Psalm 19. It includes the seventh recurrence of God's personal name, Yahweh (Lord). It represents the full shift from the ambiguous "speech" of the heavens (vv. 1–4) to the clear spoken words delivered by the transformed psalmist (v. 14). What change has occurred because of God's gift of the Torah? The psalmist is able to add his or her voice to the chorus of creation. The world comes to know Yahweh through the testimony of transformed men and women.

What is the means of transformation? It is God working in the human heart through direct encounter with God's gift of Scripture. As I've said, a transformed person is not a mechanical process. God has given us the text, but we must respond by prayerfully opening ourselves to its message. In other words, we must bring a mindset committed to a truthful engagement with God's words regardless of whether they affirm how we live or confront us in our hypocrisy. For this to happen we must steadfastly refuse to apply the words of Scripture to anyone other than us *until* we've felt the full weight of a text's implication on us. To do anything else is to become an *oppressor* rather than a *liberator*.

Once we experience deep transformation, we can then embody the good news and share it freely with others so that they too may know the life-giving truth of the Scriptures.

Verse 10 sums up the value of God's Torah for God's people. It is more valuable and desirable than *gold*. It is sweeter than *honey*. The psalmist's use of economic and culinary metaphors is worth pondering. *Gold* equals money, security, and power. A cynical view of the world might observe this: if you have *gold* to throw at a problem, you no longer have a problem. *Honey* adds flavor to otherwise bland-tasting food. It brings pleasure and joy to our lives. In the twenty-first century, we are too immersed in artificial flavors and the overconsumption of sugar to appreciate the desirability of honey. It is much easier for most of us to grasp the economic metaphor. But both put together packed a wallop for the psalmist. *Torah* is even more attractive, desirable, and delectable than money, security, power, and pure sweetness.

This is clearly counterintuitive to human experience. How many of us would choose Scripture over *gold* or *delicious food*? In our twenty-first-century world, we have grown weary of hype and marketing promises. Verse 10 sounds like something we'd hear in an infomercial or from a social media influencer. But here's the difference: *Scripture is the real deal.* Its message is valuable beyond measure, and it shows us the way to what our souls truly desire—a deep inner cleansing and a wholeness that allows our full participation in God's mission. It draws us in the same way that a pile of gold or bottle of honey would draw us. It is the true source of security and enjoyment. The difference is this: it provides its riches for all eternity.

Torah is typically translated "law" or "instruction" in modern English. Neither word captures the force of Torah properly. The word "law" sounds stuffy and remote. Law also makes us think about the legal realm or the court. Law easily morphs into legalism or a literalism that stifles the spirit behind a law. Likewise, "instruction" is problematic. Most people view instructions as options or suggestions. We can take them or leave them.

Torah is neither stuffy and dead nor is it an optional instruction manual. Torah is normative teaching that is binding in a way that liberates us. It is authoritative instruction to guide us through the journey of life. We quoted earlier John Wesley's view of the Scriptures as a book that shows us the "way to heaven." The language of "way" implies movement and a journey. Torah is a map. If we just focus on core *Torah*, that is, the books of Genesis-Deuteronomy, we will find a large block of legal materials for sure, but all of the law codes are framed largely by narratives and to a lesser degree by genealogies, lists, and poems. In the Jewish tradition, *halakhah* refers to the Jewish legal tradition as the way. I like this language as a means of expanding our understanding of law. The root word *halak* means "walk." It is a lived and living tradition that helps us as we make our way through the world. It can be applied to new times and situations as they arise. One of the reasons that Scripture has stood the test of time is its resilient ability to speak truth generation to generation as well as cross-culturally.

Genesis–Deuteronomy models its ability to speak across generations through its seemingly diverse collection of stories and laws. There are tensions built into the Torah that suggest its adaptability. For example, there are two sets of the Ten Commandments (Exod 20:1–17 and Deut 5:6–21). A careful comparison of these passages demonstrates that they are virtually the same, but each has distinctives. Most prominently the Sabbath command in Deuteronomy (vv. 12–15) has expanded the list of persons and animals who cannot work (v. 14 cf. Exod 20:10), and Deuteronomy has shifted the reason for keeping Sabbath from God's model in creation (Exod 20:11) to God's deliverance of God's people from Egypt (Deut 5:16).

What is the reason for these changes? Regardless of one's critical convictions about the authorship of these books, it is clear that these passages are addressing different needs at different times. In other words, we have a model in the Torah that is not legalistic in a *mathematical way* but remains authoritative and normative through its flexibility and adaptability for addressing different times and setting. I thus prefer the language of authoritative instruction for understanding Torah.

Also, it is clear that I am using Torah as seen in Psalm 19 in an expanded sense that includes the entire Old Testament and New Testament. There is warrant for this expanded meaning even within the Psalms. Psalms 1, 19, and 119 are Torah psalms. Their function within the Psalter is not merely to affirm the authority of the Mosaic Torah (Genesis–Deuteronomy) but also to lift up the authority of the prophets and the Psalms. Psalm 1 is a powerful text that invites the *righteous person* to live by means of a steady and continuous meditation on the Torah of Yahweh (Cf. 19:7–10 and all of Psalm 119). But Psalm 1 itself is a quilt made up of quotations from other parts of the Old Testament. Even its core teaching of meditating on the law of the Lord day and night is drawn from elsewhere (Josh 1:8).[15] The implication is that over time Israel recognized that Torah included the books of

---

15   See Brian D. Russell, "Psalm 1 as an Interpreter of Scripture" *Irish Biblical Studies* 26, no. 6 (2005): 170–93.

Moses as well as the Prophets and Writings. Jesus reflected his contemporaries by referring to the Scriptures as "the law of Moses, the prophets, and the psalms" (Luke 24:44). Paul echoed this belief in 2 Timothy 3:16. For us as Christians, Scripture now includes the Old and New Testaments. The recognition of the authority of the New Testament finds its earliest witness within its own writings. In 2 Peter 3:15–16, the writer clearly implies that Paul's letters were being read as Scripture.

What are the implications of reading Scripture as author-itative instruction or as the way? First, it reminds us that life is about growth and movement. We are not static beings. As we live and move and grow, we will encounter new situations. Even the most faithful among us run into challenges and ob-stacles as we seek to follow Jesus. The Christian life is about faith and practice. It has never been about mere *right* belief. Orthodoxy and orthopraxy go hand in hand. To separate them or to overplay either element is to no longer be Christian in any sense of the word. Right practice without grounding belief and trust lacks clarity and direction, but right belief without practice is, as James said, "dead" (James 2:26).

Jesus never said, "Believe in me" when he called disciples. Rather he said, "Follow me, and I will make you fish for people" (Matt 4:19). Jesus tied right practice specifically to missional movement. The "follow" language fits perfectly with thinking about Torah or Scripture as the "way." In my previous work, I've described a way of reading Scripture that recognizes our need for ongoing *realignment* with Jesus as we seek to follow him.[16] We read Scripture as the Way because as we journey through the world, we will from time to time find ourselves out of alignment with Jesus. Navigation is never perfect. Any vehicle using GPS will be slightly off course at any given moment. But the GPS will guide us to our destination because it continually adjusts our course in light of the conditions of the journey. Scripture is ever new in the sense that it will continue to speak to us on each step of our journey. Sometimes its voice will affirm our current actions. Other times its message will challenge us to change.

Second, Scripture as the Way or as authoritative instruction implies the need for ongoing study and interpretation. It is never enough merely to affirm or parrot the readings of prior generations or to apply them woodenly to new contexts. As we follow Jesus into the world, Scripture guides us. We must continue to read it with an openness to astonishment. Listen to its voice attentively and reflect on how it calls us to love God and neighbor in deeper and more profound ways as we find ourselves in new situations and with new questions. In fact we learn the way of Jesus through the teaching of Scripture.

Third, it is critical to read Scripture as a means of shaping us for the journey. The temptation, as we've noted, is to read Scripture for others or more often *against* others. As we follow Jesus, we need to turn the lens on ourselves. We must allow Scripture to peer within and penetrate us with its life-giving power. We always have room to grow deeper in love. The twin temptations of idolatry and injustice will always lure us from

16   See Brian Russell, *(Re)Aligning with God: Reading Scripture for Church and World* (Eugene, OR: Cascade Books, 2016), 1–7.

our commitments. We need to listen to the text and realign with its message continually as a means of living our lives as an unfolding adventure with God.

Last, God continues to speak through Scripture today. Yet even more profoundly, the Scripture itself speaks of Jesus, who in the New Testament not only fulfills Scripture and gives it its authoritative meaning but becomes the Word itself (John 1:1) to show us God (1:18). During Jesus' post-resurrection meeting with his disciples in Luke 24:36–49, Jesus "opened their minds to understand the scriptures" (v. 45). What does this mean? Jesus showed them how the Scriptures pointed to his life, death, and resurrection as well as to the mission of disciples to proclaim repentance and forgiveness in Jesus' name (v. 47). The heavens certainly declare the glory of the Creator God. Yet the Scripture ultimately reveals who this God is and tells the story not merely of the God who stands behind all reality but of the God who became flesh and walked among us as Jesus.

Questions for Reflection

- How does God speak to you through creation and through Scripture?

- How has your study of Scripture revealed your need for a deeper encounter with God?

Chapter Seven:
Scripture as a Two-Edged Sword

The models explored in the previous chapters all have strengths and weaknesses. If you've followed closely, you may have noticed that I'm most concerned about calling "time" on modes of reading that negate the power of the text on us. When I was younger, we used to do "sword" drills in my church.[17] In essence, this meant learning biblical facts and being able to recite verses. Scripture was our weapon for defeating the enemies of faith.

As I've gotten older, I've realized that the fiercest enemy to my faith is not some external foe. I am my most dangerous enemy. Therefore, I still believe in sword drills, but for me this now means falling on my own sword rather than turning it on another.

Solzenitsyn wrote, "If only it were all so simple. If only there were evil people somewhere insidiously committing evil deeds, and it were necessary only to separate them from the rest

---

17   "Sword drills" were well intended and found their roots in Paul's imagery in Eph 6:10–17.

of us and destroy them. But the line dividing good and evil cuts through the heart of every human being. And who is willing to destroy a piece of his own heart?"[18]

Hebrews 4:12 reads, "Indeed, the word of God is living and active, sharper than any two-edged sword, piercing until it divides soul from spirit, joints from marrow; it is able to judge the thoughts and intentions of the heart."

I'll step up and say that I'm willing to undergo the surgery required to shape me into the person God created me to be. I don't say this lightly. I love Solzenitsyn's words because the temptation is always to think that we have made it and only see the flaws in others. A more honest view of the world recognizes our lostness and brokenness in light of God's love.

When we recognize our deep flaws, we are ready to fall on the sword. But instead of ending our existence, God's double-edged sword performs a healing surgery on the parts of ourselves that hinder us from growing in the love of God and neighbor. Instead of marking our end, we rise up, renewed and ready to embody faith, love, and hope.

This transformation happens by exposing our fragile selves to the text. Once we've experienced the text calling us on all of the *manure* in our lives, we become ready to engage others in love. Taking a deep dive with God has shown me the uncertainties, doubts, hypocrisy, and mixed motives in my life. Yet in spite of my woundedness, I've found grace and healing through the work of God.

---

18 Aleksandr Solzhenitsyn, *The Gulag Archipelago, 1918–1956*, vol. 1 (New York: Harper and Row, 1973), 168.

God's revealing of the double mindedness inside of me has helped me to dial down my "quick to judge others" impulses. Jesus understood this reality and taught: Why do you see the speck in your neighbor's eye, but do not notice the log in your own eye? Or how can you say to your neighbor, "Let me take the speck out of your eye," while the log is in your own eye? You hypocrite, first take the log out of your own eye, and then you will see clearly to take the speck out of your neighbor's eye (Matt 7:3–5).

I have come to recognize that there is a log in my own eye. I don't want to remove it so that I can point out the specks in the eyes of others. I want to get rid of the log in my eye so that I can grow in my capacity to love God, love neighbor, and love myself. I want to be an ambassador of God's grace to others, not a judge. I'll leave the judging to God.

When we expose ourselves to the two-edged sword, we must not fear what will be exposed. It takes courage on our part and trust. I think about God's words to Joshua: Be strong and courageous (see Josh 1:6–9). God exhorted Joshua to have the courage to read Scripture and live it out. There is a gap between obedience and its outcome. When we take the decision to listen to Scripture, allow it to perform its cutting away of our inner junk, and live out its message, we will find ourselves in an odd space. It takes courage to move into uncertainty and a new way of life. Courage moves us to action, but faith sustains us in the space between action and its outcome. We need to be willing to allow Scripture to take us to new places. Such exploration is not easy, but we must learn to sit in any discomfort that exposing ourselves to Scripture creates.

Let's be clear. I'm not suggesting a move toward an individualistic piety with no outward engagement. I'm not calling for navel-gazing for navel-gazing's sake. It is for the mission of loving God so that we can more profoundly love others. Paradoxically, when God awakens us to the complexity and swamplands of our own souls, we are ready to be of use to others. We will no longer see others in a singular fashion. We will not reduce another to their family of origin, ethnicity, job description, theological commitments, political persuasion, label du jour, or their scarlet letter earned from their most public sin or association. Instead, we will see others as God sees them—complex and inwardly contorted image bearers who need grace, forgiveness, and love just as desperately as we do.

We need the Bible for all of the reasons we've explored. Scripture is what it appears to be. What's in it is what God desired to be there.

Our job is to show up and pay attention. God's Spirit continues to use Scripture for deep transformation. When we expose our bellies to its double-edged blade in earnest prayer, we will never be the same. We will come face-to-face with who we truly are and discover that God loves us anyway.

In response to this self-knowledge, we can join the desert fathers of ages past who prayed following the model of the Pharisee in Luke 18:13 by uttering the Jesus Prayer: "Lord Jesus Christ, Son of God, have mercy on me, *a sinner.*"

Along with "Lord, astonish me anew with the riches of your Word," the Jesus Prayer is one of those prayers that God will always answer. Try it out for yourself today.

Reflection Activity

Before we move deeper into our conversation with Scripture, I'd invite you to think through your present understanding and beliefs about the Bible. Grab a sheet of paper and write out a series of affirmations or truths that describe your current beliefs about Scripture and how you hope to relate to it.

As an example, here are some of my maxims for reading and living out the text:

Scripture is an ever-flowing stream and replenishes us when/if we ask God to astonish us as we read it.

Scripture is endlessly interesting when we remain mindful enough to ponder it deeply and listen attentively.

When reading Scripture, don't pray for mastery of the text; pray that the text masters you.

Reading Scripture requires that we approach the text as its servant rather than its master.

It's not about fitting the Bible into my life; it's about fitting my life into the biblical story.

Reading Scripture is not ultimately about bringing our questions to the text; it is about opening ourselves up to the questions that the text desires to ask of us.

Reading Scripture invites us to the true world that God desires for us to inhabit and work toward in our lives together.

Reading Scripture is not a means of self-actualization; it is a means of personal conversion to God.

Don't let go of biblical text until God reveals in it how to reciprocate God's love for us as well as channel love to those around us.

Now it's your turn. Write out your ideas about how Scripture works in your life.

Part Two:
Opening Ourselves Fully to God's Word

Chapter Eight:
Idolatherapy

———— · ◦ ◉ ◦ · ————

First John ends abruptly. John warns, "Little children, keep your-
selves from idols" (5:21). The odd thing about John's warning is
that he doesn't mention idols or idolatry by name anywhere else
in his letter. John's final exhortation invites us to go back and
reread his words as a warning against idolatry. More profoundly,
it speaks to the ubiquitous nature of idols in the first century.
They were everywhere. Each city had its own deities. Each house-
hold had its favorite gods and goddesses. Any reading of the New
Testament from Acts to Revelation informs the reader of the
issues of false worship as well as ethical dilemmas faced by early
believers, such as meat sacrificed to other gods. The danger for us
today is we think that we've evolved past idolatry and paganism.
In truth, we haven't progressed much at all. John Calvin's words
from "Christian" Geneva remain true: "the human mind is, so to
speak, a perpetual forge of idols."[19] We may not worship actual

---

19   John Calvin, *Institutes of the Christian* Religion, trans. Henry Beveridge (Grand
     Rapids: Eerdmans, 1989), 97. This line is sometimes translated "the human
     mind is an idol factory."

idols, but we still worship and serve the same realities behind the literal idols of our ancestors.

"I'm Brian Russell and I'm a recovering polytheist."

The students in my classroom always looked stunned when I dropped this line. What was their professor saying to them? Was he confessing some secret sin? Had he lost his faith or possibly his mind? But I was serious that day. I still am today.

The more that I read the Bible, the less certain I am about the undivided nature of my heart. Or to be blunt, I am increasingly certain about the divided nature of my heart. What do I mean?

It's simple. I struggle with precisely the same issues that Israel repeatedly faced. Israel struggled to love the Lord and to love others. In other words, they faced the twin challenges of idolatry and injustice. Idolatry is the opposite of loving the Lord; injustice is the opposite of loving our neighbor. God sent the prophets of old to call Israel back to its Torah roots.

Two powerful declarations summarize all of the teachings of Moses in Genesis to Deuteronomy:

"Love your neighbor as yourself." (Lev 19:18b)

"Hear, O Israel: [Yahweh] is our God, [Yahweh] alone. You shall love [Yahweh] your God with all your heart and with all your soul and with all your might." (Deut 6:4–5)

[Jesus said,] "On these two commandments hang all the law and prophets." (Matt 22:40)

If you've been a Christian for any amount of time, it's likely you already know about these two commandments. But I want to suggest that there is more here for you. In this chapter, I will take us on a deep dive into these commandments.

By the end of the chapter, you will know why I consider idolatry and syncretism to be the major impediments to our growth in grace. You will have tools for exploring your own heart and locating blocks, attitudes, and beliefs that run contrary to the Gospel. You will feel more integrated in your head, heart, and hands. You will gain confidence in the power of Scripture to transform you in the deepest parts of your being.

The biggest hindrance to our growth in grace and personal witness is our denial of the idolatry in our lives. One of the tragedies of the success of the Church in the Western world is that the triumph of monotheism has hidden the reality of gods and goddesses all around us.

Brian, are you saying that there really are other gods? Yes. But listen carefully to the distinction that I'm about to make. The God of Scripture is *unique*. The God of the Bible is *transcendent*. I don't like to overuse technical terms, but *transcendence* is a critical concept for us to engage.

When we confess with Deuteronomy 6:4 that the "Lord is our God, the Lord is our one and only,"[20] we are confessing the uniqueness and incomparability of God in contrast to all other beings and things. The God of Scripture stands outside of creation. In other words, God may not be identified with any

---

20 For this translation, see R. W. L. Moberly, *Old Testament Theology: Reading the Hebrew Bible as Christian Scripture* (Ada, MI: Baker Academic, 2013), 7–40.

being or aspect of creation itself. God is the creator of all that is, was, and will be.

Modern science continues to make astonishing discoveries about the vastness and complexity of the universe both at the macro and micro levels. The subatomic levels of reality mirror the complexity of the virtual infinite nature of the universe. Yet to speak of the God of Scripture, we must imagine a being who is capable not only of wrapping thought and understanding around all that is but being the creator force behind it. That is transcendence.

Even if the universe were to cease to exist, God would still be. God is not a rock, a person, a flower, a planet, an idea, or anything within the created realm. This is the essence of transcendence. God stands outside of time and space.

How does the idea of transcendence relate to our understanding idolatry and injustice? Idolatry is about divided loyalty. The key shift in our spiritual growth is recognizing that the Lord alone is worthy of our full committed loyalty because of who God is. God is qualitatively different from creation because God is the creator.

Our ultimate loyalty is to the creator, not to any part of creation. Idolatry is the false elevation of any value, god, person, idea, or thing to the level of creator.

My wife's name is Astrid. She is the love of my life. We are soul partners and have committed to love, honor, and support one another. Our relationship is *exclusive* to us. This is the essence of faithfulness in monogamy.

Both of us have friends, acquaintances, and work relationships with others. But these relationships are qualitatively different because they exist on a lower level than our marital relationship. To be faithful to Astrid, I cannot have relationships with any other person on the same emotional and physical intimacy level that Astrid and I share. To do so would be adulterous.

Scripture throughout its pages portrays idolatry as spiritual adultery. Most famously the book of Hosea illustrates the problem of idolatry in Israel by highlighting the marriage of the prophet to an unfaithful woman named Gomer. Hosea and Gomer serve as visible metaphors of the relationship between the Lord and God's people. In other words, idolatry involves *infidelity* or a lack of faithfulness. This is spiritual adultery.

Too often we think of idolatry as the complete rejection of God. This is rarely the case and is the reason why *adultery* and *infidelity* are such good descriptors of the type of idolatry found in the Old Testament. An unfaithful spouse or partner does not always intend to leave the relationship. Instead, he or she attempts to have it both ways.

It's the same with religion. Few of us will outright reject Jesus as Lord. The problem is that we tend to worship Jesus alongside our conscious and unconscious commitments to other gods and goddesses. Take a look at the Old Testament. Israel didn't stop worshipping the Lord. They simply worshipped the Lord along with worshipping Baal, Asherah, and other deities.

The problem is that the God of the Bible isn't just another deity. The God of Scripture (Father, Son, and Holy Spirit) is the Creator of all that exists. This means that God is even the creator of the "gods." God is not merely the organizer of preexisting material, nor is God under the influence of impersonal forces. Both of these realities are true in worldviews that lack transcendence. The gods of the nations around Israel were almost innumerable. There were gods of war, peace, wine, storms, the underworld, revelry, fertility, family, trees, the sun, the moon, animals, love, joy, wisdom, and the list goes on. In other words, the gods at their core represented actual aspects of reality.

When we fail to recognize that the "gods" are real, we set ourselves up for an unconscious syncretism. We deny idolatry because we deny the existence of the "gods." Yet we fool ourselves because our denial is merely at the semantic level. We've failed to get at the heart issue: the denial of the existence of other gods is not the same as a *desire* for only King Jesus.

How do we change our desires? As soon as we ask this question, we are beginning to get at the true heart of what reading Scripture for transformation is all about. Remember Augustine's goal for interpretation? He said that we as readers are not finished until we have the capacity to "build up this double love of God and neighbor." Augustine wants more than knowledge or proper teaching. The mark of understanding is the transformation of Christians into embodiments of the commandments to love God and neighbor. The end result is men and women who model faith, hope, and love (1 Cor 13:13).

Augustine does a deep dive into what this love looks like. He references 1 Timothy 1:5 more than any other biblical text in his *On Christian Teaching*[21]: "But the aim of such instruction

---

21   Four times: 20, 27, 29, and 144 (see intro., n. 1).

is love that comes from a pure heart, a good conscience, and sincere faith." Listen carefully to Augustine:

> For when the apostle said "love" he added "from a pure heart," so that nothing is loved except what should be loved. He added "good" to "conscience" because of hope; for a person with the incubus of a bad conscience despairs of reaching what he loves and believes. Thirdly, he said "with a genuine faith":[22] for if our faith is free of untruthfulness then we do not love what should not be loved, whereas by living aright it is impossible for our hope to be in any way misguided.[23]

The key to reaching the heights of which Augustine speaks turns on our openness to deep transformation in reading the text. We need a way of studying the Bible that opens our whole being to the illumination of God's Word. In what follows I'm going to share a way of reading that I call *idolatherapy*. If our principal issue is idolatry and syncretism, we need an interpretive method designed specifically to address the blocks to the transformation Augustine and we want to see in the lives of pastors and everyday believers.

Can we truly love what ought to be loved? Can we live with a good and clean conscience? Can our faith be undivided and grounded fully in truth?

I believe that the answer is yes. But I write in the full recognition of my frailties, weaknesses, and inner complexity. Yet

---

22   NRSV reads "a sincere faith."

23   Augustine, *On Christian Teaching*, 29.

I don't write in despair. The work of growth in love is the work of all eternity. I believe in the ability of God's grace through the Spirit to transform me *noticeably, substantially,* and *profoundly* in this life. I also recognize my present position as "chief of sinners" (see 1 Tim 1:15).

Augustine hints at a core problem in the passage quoted above. He describes a life where "nothing is loved except what should be loved." In *You Are What You Love: The Power of Habit,* James K. A. Smith writes, "We are what we want. Our wants and longings and desires are at the core of our identity, the wellspring from which our actions and behavior flow."[24] The issue according to Smith is that we may not love the people and things that we *think* we love.

We can read Scripture for a lifetime, but if our *desires* remain unchanged, there will be no true growth in love. I had a conversation on my *Deep Dive Spirituality Conversations* podcast in 2020 with Dr. J. R. Woodward.[25] In part, we discussed the formative practices critical for helping church planters to grow spiritually. Woodward resisted offering a cookie-cutter checklist. He believes that it is just as important to discern the practices that are deforming us. He suggested that it was perhaps more critical to observe a person's life over the course of a couple of days than it was to proscribe a certain Bible reading program or a set number of minutes in daily prayer.

---

24   James K. A. Smith, *You Are What You Love* (Grand Rapids: Brazos, 2016), 112.

25   Brian Russell, *The Deep Dive Spirituality Conversations Podcast,* "Episode 32: Dr JR Woodward: Identity, Spiritual Formation, and the Shaping of Missional Leaders," November 4, 2020, https://deepdivespirituality.podbean.com/e/episode-32-dr-jr-woodward-identity-spiritual-formation-and-the-shaping-of-missional-leaders/.

Imagine a drone following us around for week that filmed and recorded our every move and action. What would we learn about what was actually shaping us spiritually? What would we uncover about our true commitments and values? What are we reading outside of Scripture? What are we listening to while driving our cars? Which television shows and movies do we consume? With whom do we spend our time? What are our hobbies? How do we spend our money?

When we begin to explore these questions, it becomes easier to understand why our typical spiritual practices (if we have consistent ones) often bear little fruit. I can read Scripture daily, but its voice can easily be lost in the chorus of noise in modern life. If I am not careful, the message of Scripture can easily find itself co-opted by modern ideologies of the right, left, or center, or by the allure of consumerism, security, and personal afflu-ence, or by our inner unhealed wounds. We end up "mirror" reading. In other words, instead of Scripture shaping us, we find our personal reflection in its words, and so we simply remain as we were before we read it. In other words, the Bible even if read consistently can have little or no influence on our core desires.

Now, I will be the first to recognize that we are talking about a complex topic. All of us have blind spots and miss aspects of meaning in a text due to our inherent biases. These biases are the result of nature and nurture. Our sex and gender influence how we read. Our ethnicity and socioeconomic status play a role in our perception of meaning. Our theological commitments blind us to some insights and make others completely obvious. Our dis-positions influence how we read. Some of us are naturally positive in outlook, and our readings of Scripture can easily slide in an upbeat direction. Others of us are more solemn by nature and our interpretations tend in that direction. Entire denominations exist due to subtle differences in reading. In our present context, there is a deep divide between Christians over political ideology. Some read the Scripture as a support to a leftward tilt toward more collectivist solutions; others read the Bible in ways that parrot libertarian and more individualistic policies.

Truth be told, we are a mix of true and false readings. The challenge is establishing limits and boundaries regarding what a text *meant* in its original context and what a text *means* to us (whoever "us" is) today. The challenge for us who are committed to deep transformation is that we ironically need to learn to *distrust* our gut instincts as a means of combating our biases. Readings are often tribal. If I am honest, I have to admit to enjoying reading commentators and exegetes who agree with my perspective on the text. I like the affirmation that this brings to my work. When I find affirming readings, I feel as though Jesus is saying to me, "You are not far from the kingdom." Yet I want to suggest that our capacity for deep transformation rests on our ability to push beyond easy readings that only affirm our current beliefs. In fact, I'd suggest that we would be better off as God's people if we developed an initial skepticism about any interpretation that doesn't call us to *change* and *repentance.* In my own life, I've learned to pay careful attention to the elements of texts that I find challenging to my life. If we are not intentional, we can fall into the habit of finding *interesting things* in the Bible rather than cultivating an *interest in* how the Bible calls our lives and values into question.

The Church is always at its weakest when it finds itself co-opted by cultural pressures. During such times, we naively equate the values of our culture or preferred ideological positions with the values of Christianity. This co-opting happens to believers across the political spectrum and is one of the most divisive and pressing issues facing God's people today.

We need to cultivate a reading strategy that can consistently put the spotlight on our biased interpretations and call us on our personal/tribal shibboleths and "bravo sierra" (bs). Such a strategy is not a pleasant form of reading because it does not bring immediate comfort. In fact, it's quite uncomfortable because one will feel significantly less holy and self-righteous when it's done correctly. The good news, however, is that the Spirit seems to honor such readings, and it will bear fruit in our lives in terms of deep growth in grace. Just as importantly, others will see the changes in you. As disciples committed to making disciples, our witness and ability to reach others must always be in the forefront of our minds.

I call this way of reading for spiritual formation *idolatherapy*. In case it's not obvious, this is a made-up word by me that combines *idolatry* and *therapy*. I've talked about *idolatry* and *syncretism* previously and the deep threats that they pose to loving God and neighbor. I prefer to add the word *therapy* because of our context in the twenty-first century. Ours is a therapeutic culture. Whether we like it or not, we live in the awareness of the power of the unconscious. We can talk about the false self and shadow when we discuss our identity. Cutting-edge neuroscience can explain many behaviors biologically.

My hope is that reading the Bible through a lens of idolatherapy will lead you to substantive breakthroughs that God's Spirit can use to cleanse you at the core of your being. When you experience this cleansing, you will be freer to love God and others in even more profound ways than you presently do. You will lose the illusion of your innocence as well as your self-righteousness. You will also suddenly stop blaming external circumstances or people alone for your present reality. Scripture will begin to show you truths that you likely need to hear. The process isn't always pleasant, but it is healing. It's not only good for you; it is good for those closest to you and for the watching world.

Idolatherapy is code for ripping off the bandages that mask our wounds, disordered desires, sins, and other illusions that prevent God's grace from doing its deepest work. When we truly allow Scripture into our inner world, we will begin to experience the transformation that we long for. If you are a pastor or teacher, you have the privilege of being the first convert to this type of reading. Then you can model it for those whom you have the privilege of serving.

The following chapters in this section of the book will develop the idea of idolatherapy into an actionable reading method for you and for those with whom you read the Bible.

Questions for Reflection

- How has this chapter changed the way you think about the meaning of idolatry?

- What blind spots do you sense may be hindering your ability to hear God's word and change in light of it?

- What interests you about the idea of idolatherapy? What questions do you have about it?

Chapter Nine:
The Danger of Disordered Desires

———— · · ● · · ————

If you are a pastor, you've likely heard of the need to separate your devotional life from your regular engagement with the Bible for sermon preparation or teaching. If you are a layperson, you may be surprised to learn about this idea. Such advice is well intended. It is important for pastors and spiritual leaders to recognize our need for spiritual enrichment apart from the *work* of the ministry. But the mistake in doing this is that we can *sanitize* Scripture by making it an object of study. We interpret it with the goal of a sermon for *others.* By the way, lay readers also face the temptation of thinking about others who need to hear the text we are reading. In the previous chapter, I mentioned the necessity of being the first convert to the text. I now want to explore a helpful grid of areas in which Scripture will, over the course of time, engage our way of life.

In the third and fourth centuries, the Christian monastic movement began. Men and women seeking a deeper life retreated from society to remote regions of Egypt and Syria.

These persons practiced a disciplined life of denial out of a love for Christ. Perhaps surprisingly, they faced vigorous tests during their periods of solitude and full surrender to God. In their pursuit of purification in love, they confronted "demons" that they thought that they'd left behind. One of the most well-know of the early monks was St. Anthony. For example, he reportedly battled heroically against what he called a demon of lust.

The fourth-century monastic Evagrius Ponticus isolated what he termed "Eight Evil Thoughts" that men and women living in solitude would likely experience.[26] Over time, these eight thoughts became the roots of what we now know as the seven deadly sins. I find Evagrius' categories to be of enduring value. They emerged out of the lives of persons deeply committed to Jesus and growth in grace. For our purposes, they can serve as filters for our growth through the reading of Scripture.

In popular culture, the "seven deadly sins" are descriptions of the actions and domain of sinners. But for those of us hungry for the depths of God's love and grace, they are parts of ourselves that remain unsurrendered to God. During those times when Scripture seems dry or irrelevant or a struggle to read, we may discover that the obstacles to our growth are the deforming thoughts that Evagrius named for us.

The most basic questions for idolatherapy are these:

- What is preventing me from loving God?
- What hinders my ability to love my neighbor as myself?

---

26 Evagrius Ponticus, *The Praktikos and Chapters on Prayer*, Cistercian Studies Series 4, translated and with an introduction and notes by John Eudes Bamberger (Trappist, KY: Cistercian Publications, 1972), 15–26.

- Moreover, what is blocking me from being able to fully embody the words I find in Scripture?

As we've hinted at in our reflection in earlier chapters, the answers are that we have *loves* in our lives that run counter to our theological and biblical commitments. They sit in the depths of our inner world. When confronted, they fight back against us as though they were external forces. When I read of St. Anthony's battles with demons in the desert, I don't doubt the reality of his struggles, but I understand his struggle as essentially a deep confrontation with his inner world and desires.

Our loves apart from loving God and loving neighbor can easily become *disordered desires.* It is important to clarify the meaning of the phrase. To desire someone or something is not a sin. The key distinction is that a desire can become *disordered* when we become so attached to it that it begins to control us or to distract us from our true aim in life: love for God and love for neighbor. In essence, the disordered desires are manifestations of idolatry and injustice and hinder us from growth in love.

Here is Evagrius's list: gluttony, impurity/lust, avarice/greed, sadness, anger, sloth, vainglory, and pride. When we read Scripture, we will likely have to face these *disordered desires* on the pathway to deep transformation. Reading Scripture well involves recognizing that we will learn things about our inner world that we'd prefer not to know. Reading Scripture will sometimes paint a disturbing picture of us that we may resist. The death of idols in our lives will always be painful. False gods and goddesses do not die an easy death.

On the pathway to wholeness in Christ, we will have to navigate these distracting thoughts. The challenge is to allow

Scripture to confront us before applying it to others. Here's a not-so-fun lesson that I've learned as I've gotten older. Whenever I read a text and it immediately brings to mind someone else who needs to be practicing its message, it's actually a signal that the someone is I. To be the first convert to a text involves the painful process of idolatherapy.

Gandhi is famously credited with saying, "Be the change that you want to see in the world." It is a powerful counterbalance to a world that expects "on demand" service or immediate justice. Sanctification is the work of a lifetime. Yes, there are moments of deep insight and transformation. But growth in love takes time and will be ongoing likely for all eternity. How can we ever exhaust our ability to love God, others, or self at ever higher levels? Of course, we'd love to snap our fingers and see our world reflect the values of God's kingdom. We long to see others "acting justly, loving mercy, and walking humbly with God" as the prophet Micah summarized God's desires for humanity (see Micah 6:8). But the work starts in the inner world of each of us.

Learn to focus on modeling the life of God. This only happens by turning our attention to our response to grace. It's the only aspect of change over which we have any control. Have the courage to open yourself to God's work.

We'll now explore Evagrius' eight distracting thoughts: gluttony, lust, greed, sadness, anger, spiritual sloth, vainglory, and pride. We need to be attuned to these as we read Scripture. They may arise and block our hearing of the word by deflecting our focus from its cutting edge.

Each of these thoughts is likely to be encountered as we seek to grow in grace. Wise readers of Scripture will be attuned to their seduction and turn back to the Word when we recognize one or more of them singing their siren song deep within us.

The distracting thoughts are not the idols that need to be removed per se. They represent our inner soul's vanguard that attempts to block the Spirit's work in our life.

Too many Christians mistake the distracting thoughts for the sins themselves. We assume that thoughts of sin are the same as actual sinning. Yes, I fully understand the role that fantasy can play, and there is clearly a line at which an obsession with a thought moves into the realm of sin. But we must remember Martin Luther's humorous adage: "We can't stop a bird from landing in our tree, but we don't have to permit it to build a nest." Paul exhorts us to "take every thought captive" (2 Cor 10:5). We do this one thought or feeling at a time. Any time that we become aware of one of these thoughts, it is an invitation to return anew to our loving Lord.

But here's a hard-earned truth. If we *feel* guilt or shame because of an impure thought that enters our mind, we actually give it more power than it deserves. Learn to recognize the distracting thoughts for what they are—visitors from our unconscious. We can slowly constrict them of the oxygen that they need to thrive simply by releasing them to God when they arise rather than feeling bad that they appeared in our minds. We will never get to the deep work of growth in love if we stay at the surface level of our thoughts. Learn to use a prayer word or phrase to recenter: "Lord, hear my prayer" or "Jesus" or use the ancient Jesus Prayer: "Lord Jesus Christ, Son of God, have mercy on me a sinner."[27]

You may be wondering why I'm spending time on Evagrius's eight distracting thoughts in a book on how to read the Bible for deep transformation. Here is the reason: reading Scripture will remain at a surface or intellectual level *until* we recognize the blocks in our hearts to the Spirit's work. Reading Scripture at the deeper levels requires more than mere knowledge or technique. Our highest contribution is our willingness to surrender continually and courageously to the work of the Spirit. What hinders the work of the Spirit? Evagrius named them for us. Let's dive into the specifics.

Confronting the Eight Distracting Thoughts

Level 1: Survival Instincts

The first three of the distracting thoughts are disordered desires about survival: sustenance, sex, and security. These three form a triad that all persons must learn to gain mastery over through surrender lest they master us. Their underlying desire are keys to the continuation of human life in the world, but left unchecked, they can throw us off-balance and blind us to our true need for God and God's grace. God created us with brains wired for our personal survival and for the survival of our species. In other words, God gave us, as human beings, the

---

27   You can use various iterations of the Jesus Prayer as well: "Lord Jesus Christ, Son of God, have mercy" or "Lord Jesus Christ, Son of God, have mercy on me your child." The key is simply finding a way to return to our moment-by-moment walk with the God who loves us. For a deeper dive, see Brian Russell, *Centering Prayer: Sitting Quietly in God's Presence Can Change Your Life* (Brewster, MA: Paraclete, 2021), 113–44.

desire for food for sustenance; sex for connectedness, pleasure, and for creating the next generation; and a stress response to threats to our security and existence. But these natural and good dimensions of human life can take a darker turn that act *against* us rather than for us.

Gluttony refers to a focus around our need for food or even becoming overly concerned with our health. Overeating is the textbook illustration of gluttony, but it is only one manifestation of gluttony. In the developed world, especially in the United States, many do struggle with consuming too many calories in their diets. From a spiritual perspective, the feeling of hunger can distract us from our work of listening to Scripture. Moreover, an obsession with our overall health can block a deeper encounter with God. We can be overly focused on fitness or a particular diet, or we can be frightened or concerned about a health condition. Jesus dealt swiftly with the distraction of gluttony during his forty days in the wilderness. When the devil tempted Jesus to satisfy his hunger by transforming stones into bread, Jesus turned to Scripture for help. He quoted Deuteronomy: "One does not live by bread alone, but by every word that comes from the mouth of the Lord" (8:3 cf. Matt 4:4).

Jesus' reaction to Satan models for us how to turn any obstacle to our growth into an opportunity. Yes, Jesus was hungry. He had been fasting. But rather than focusing on the distraction of gluttony, he returned to the Scripture for true sustenance. As we move to a deep idolatherapy, we prepare ourselves for the word by moving past the distracting thoughts about our hunger, present health, or mere survival.

Impurity/lust is the disordered expression of natural sexual desire. Sex is one of the most pleasurable gifts that God has given to us. Many Christians struggle with sex and rightly so because it so often has been taught as something dirty or bad. The early church for a variety of reasons privileged chastity as a higher calling and recognized marriage as acceptable but not the ideal. The influence of Augustine has been strong. His spiritual classic *Confessions* traces his journey to a conversion to Christianity. A key element of his transformation involved his deliverance from lust and fornication and the embrace of chastity as the mark of his conversion. In the Western church, shame and guilt have always lurked around our understanding of sexuality. Pornography and lust are evident in our wider culture. Pastors and persons committed to Christ struggle in these areas too.

Yet sexual thoughts are natural. They become disordered only when they become obsessive. For example, one may naturally notice another person and feel a sense of attraction. But one doesn't have to let it morph into unbridled lust. The danger of disordered sexual desire is that it *depersonalizes* another by turning him or her merely into an object of our desire for sexual release.

As we come to Scripture, we must recognize the power of our sexual impulses. On one hand, they are natural. We were born to reproduce. We will find ourselves attracted to others. We will feel sexual desire. The key is how we respond to its energy. Our sexual energy cannot merely be handled for the long haul through denial of its existence or through the suppression of its reality. It is a natural part of life for singles and couples. The cure for lust is not marriage, nor is it mere ascetic self-denial. Many Christians marry early. Later in life some admit that they desired sex or went too far during their courtship and felt obligated because of the release of sexual energy.

The cure for lust is recognizing its presence and turning to God in a posture of trust that the energy can be shifted to our engagement with the Bible (we are after all reflecting on reading Scripture) or some other purpose than unbridled sexual release in any way that dehumanizes or merely objectifies another soul. Just as a concern for food or health can block us in our reading of Scripture so can a mind distracted by erotic desire. Pray: "As the deer pants for the water so my soul longs after you" and gently return to the text.

Avarice/greed is a tangible response to the fear that I do not have enough. Today it is often associated with a disordered desire for wealth. But this is too easy of an association. Yes, wealth can turn into an obsession both for those who have it but want more and for those who do not have it but desire it. Yet the issue is deeper than wealth. It is more about the false sense of power and security that wealth promises. When we feel a deep sense of lack, we desire to fill the need. The opposite of avarice is not simply generosity but rather the recognition of an abundance that brings contentment. Abundance and contentment come from a position of trust rather than fear regarding our survival. Survival and security are core human needs. Our bodies and brains react to stress with a fight-or-flight response. The impulse of survival creates a deep desire for wealth and possessions as a hedge against the fear of lack. Check your heart today. Ask: Am I worried about money? Am I fearful about the safety and security of myself and of the persons whom I love the most? Am I distracted by the lifestyle of others?

Cultivating a heart of gratitude can work consciously against greed and avarice. Scripture consistently reminds us to give thanks and make thanksgiving part of our daily life. Gratitude is one of the great antidotes to the fear of not having enough. Gratitude breeds contentment in times of plenty and times of lack. Gratitude is the enemy of entitlement. When we practice a spirit of gratitude, we turn from a fear focused on what we don't have to a sense of abundance focused on what God has given. In the process, the attractiveness of avarice and greed loses its sheen. Pray: "Astonish me anew with the *riches* of your Word."

Level 2: Dispositions of the Heart

If Evagrius's first three thoughts focused on three powerful natural drives found in all people, the second triad (sadness, anger, and sloth) are disordered dispositions of the heart. They represent strong feelings that act against our true desire to grow into the people whom God created us to be. These three are easier to shield from the perception of others, but they are no less deadly to our spiritual growth and well-being. As we move further into Evagrius' list, the power of deformation is just as threatening to our true self as the more obvious threats of gluttony, greed, and unbridled lust. In fact, you'll be surprised that Evagrius considered the deeper levels to be the most destructive to our desire for a transformed life because of their subtlety.

Sadness is not the same as clinical depression. It is also not the natural feeling of sadness experienced following a personal loss. Grieving the loss of a loved one or friend is not an "evil" thought. What Evagrius noticed was a certain melancholy present among those who had retreated into the desert with an intention to be devoted fully to God. This sadness was from a sense of a lack of spiritual attainment, or sadness over leaving one's past life only to experience immense struggle in spiritual growth.

In the modern world, we have the expression FOMO (fear of missing out). In the spiritual life, we may experience a similar distraction when we focus on what we gave up to follow Christ as well as temptation to chase after markers of spiritual maturity. Both paths can lead to a melancholy and sense of spiritual dryness that can distract us from the ongoing work that God desires to do in us.

Anger is the easiest of the second triad to describe. We've all felt the distracting power of anger. Even those who externally appear calm can inwardly simmer with thoughts of revenge and rage. The Church fathers probably wrote more about the danger of anger than any of the other distracting thoughts.[28] Anger is an emotion that creates an instant response of action. Scripture records Jesus being angry (Mark 3:1–6).[29] In the Sermon on the Mount, Jesus warned his disciples about anger (Matt 5:21–26). Paul wrote, "Be angry but do not sin; do not let the sun go down on your anger" (Eph 4:26). In the spiritual life, we will find times when we are angry. Feeling anger over an injustice or some

---

28   Roberta Bondi, *To Love as God Loves: Conversations with the Early Church* (Philadelphia: Fortress, 1987), 73–74.

29   In John 2:13–17, Jesus overturns tables and drives folks out of the temple. The word *anger* doesn't appear, but Jesus' actions seem fueled by what we would call anger.

needless tragedy is not sinful. The issue is how long does it linger. The disordered version of anger is when it becomes an obsession that we refuse to let go of. We can carry a simmering rage for a long time. I write this from personal experience. As I've opened myself up more to the work of God, God has revealed to me resentments and hurt feelings from my past. These memories will often return during encounters with Scripture. They distract us because they remind us of past hurts. So instead of hearing the Scriptures, our focus turns to old tapes and stories of past wrongs. Again, the remedy is awareness and surrender: "Lord Jesus Christ, have mercy on me." Or "Forgive us our debts, as we also have forgiven our debtors" (Matt 6:12).

Sloth is easily misunderstood in the spiritual life. Sloth is more than mere laziness. Sloth as a spiritual threat is not the opposite of ambition. The sloth that Evagrius identified is a spiritual laziness. It is present when we sense a loss of passion for the possibility and real experience of growth in grace. A good term for it is *spiritual complacency*. Tozer puts it this way: "The stiff and wooden quality about our religious lives is a result of our lack of holy desire. Complacency is a deadly foe of all spiritual growth. Acute desire must be present or there will be no manifestation of Christ to His people."[30]

Evagrius saw sloth as such a significant threat that he described spiritual sloth as the "noonday demon." We sit in sloth when we fall into the thoughts that we've gone far enough in grace. It's a type of spiritual boredom and complacency. Whenever we read Scripture and can't wait to finish, we are in the midst of spiritual sloth. When we read and think, "I already

---

30 A.W. Tozer, *The Pursuit of God* (New York: Waymark Books, 2020), 13.

understand this text," we are experiencing sloth's power. The cure for sloth is the desire for astonishment. We can combat sloth by taking on the attitude of Jacob when he hung on for dear life and demanded a blessing in his struggle with God at the river Jabbok. Also remember God's words to Joshua: "Only be strong and very courageous, being careful to act in accordance with all the law that my servant Moses commanded you; do not turn from it to the right hand or to the left, so that you may be successful wherever you go. This book of the law shall not depart out of your mouth; you shall meditate on it day and night, so that you may be careful to act in accordance with all that is written in it" (Josh 1:7–8).

Level 3: Spiritual Pride

The final two distracting thoughts (vainglory and pride) are subtle but highly destructive for those desiring deep growth in grace. Both terms are manifestations of spiritual pride. Evagrius believed from his observations of himself and others that pride is so insidious to the spiritual life that it required two related terms to capture its depth. Vainglory focuses on external praise; pride on internal praise. Both must be recognized and resisted. Otherwise, spiritual pride will slowly constrict and suffocate the work of transformation that God desires to do in us. The danger is the subtlety of pride. It appears as soon as we think: "Wow. I finally overcame the six other distracting thoughts. I've made it." Or "I hope others see what God has done in my life."

Vainglory is easy to spot. It's the desire for affirmation. Readers of the Word have to be careful about motives. The danger is that we can learn to read Scripture as a means of receiving praise rather than as a means of inner transformation and the channeling of good news to others. Vainglory also can rise in our response to praise given to others. Notice how you react when you hear a compliment or praise given to another soul. Are you genuinely happy and grateful for the recognition of the other, or are there subtle hints of jealousy within?

There is always the risk of **pride**, that is, a sense of superiority over others, as we grow spiritually. It's ironic but true. We intellectually understand that salvation is a gift, but after we receive the gift, we then hold on to it as if we were responsible for its effectiveness. As we know from reading 1 Corinthians 1–3, Christians can break into factions in which one group views themselves as more spiritual than the others. I've experienced this reality in most local churches that I've participated in. If only the rest of the Church were as committed as we are! I hear this in pastors and seminary students who feel enlightened compared with the laity whom they have the privilege to serve. I've found it in my own heart. We point to what we've done, the knowledge we've acquired, the spiritual disciplines we practice, and the experiences we've felt. We subtly shift from persons transformed by grace into persons who have made heroic transformations through our own strength. In terms of the study of the Bible, our growth can be blocked by pride. In fact, the moment we become experts on the Bible marks the day when our voice becomes the authority rather than God's. Don't pray, "Lord, help me to master this text." Instead say, "Lord, I open myself to hear all that you have for me. Master me through my conversation with your Word."

Don't let the above reflection become its own distraction. Now is not the time for self-judgment. That doesn't help. God is the judge. The good news is that God loves you unconditionally. God already knows your struggles and your strengths.

So, is a deep love for God and neighbor possible then given these distracting thoughts? Of course it is. But we have to recognize that there are no quick fixes. It is a process of cultivating habits that negate our deformation via our disordered desires.

Our habits will both make us and break us. It's fascinating to me that for all of his theological reflection on the meaning of sin and grace, Augustine focuses the blame on our individual choices. Ponder these sentences cut from an extended passage in *Confessions*:

> For my will was perverse and lust had grown from it, when I gave in to lust habit was born, and when I did not resist the habit it became a necessity. There were the links which together formed what I have called my chain and it held me fast in the duress of servitude. . . . For the rule of sin is the force of habit, by which the mind is swept along and held fast against its will, yet deservedly, because it fell into the habit of its own accord.[31]

In other words, we become what we repeatedly practice. Habits good or bad become the default actions of our lives. What we think we do. What we do we become. What we become then transforms into the default modes of our lives. These default beliefs and actions run at the unconscious level

---

31 Augustine, *Saint Augustine Confessions: A New Translation by R. S. Pine-Coffin* (Baltimore: Penguin, 1961), *bk.* 8.5, 164–65.

and can actually thwart our reading of the text and leave us struggling to live out its message.

Idolatherapy recognizes that part of learning to read the text is developing the soul awareness to confront the eight distracting thoughts when they appear. In other words, the biblical text cannot confront us fully until we've invited the Holy Spirit to do a deep cleansing of us.

In the next chapter we will peel back another layer and explore another facet of the surrendered life.

Questions for Reflection

- How often do these eight distracting thoughts surface while I am attempting hear to God speak through the study of the Bible?

- In what ways have I grown to tolerate these eight distracting thoughts in my life?

- With which of these eight distracting thoughts do I presently struggle the most?

Chapter Ten:
W(hole)ness and Scripture

· ● ● ● · ●

In this chapter, I will share a wordplay for understanding growth in grace. Through it, you will have a clear picture in your mind of the principal hindrance to growth and how Scripture can help us to open up more fully to the work God desires to do in us. My prayer is that you will experience a deeper hunger for what God's grace can accomplish in your life.

I want to go back to the word *wholeness*. Notice that the word *hole* sits within *wholeness*. Blaise Pascal is famous for arguing that "there is a God-shaped vacuum in the heart of each man which cannot be satisfied by any created thing but only by God the Creator, made known through Jesus Christ."

As I've reflected on the blocks that we erect that thwart God's work in our lives, I believe that Pascal's insight is correct. There is a hole in us that competes against our growth in wholeness. This "hole" is more like a black hole in that it seeks to pull our growth in grace back into its abyss.

What does this hole feel like? It creates many bodily sensations and goes by many names. It's our sense of lack. It's the subtle tightness we may feel in our spines or shoulder muscles. It's those anxious feelings in our abdomens. The hole is also responsible for the tapes and tracks that play in our heads. Some may sound like this: "I'm not enough" or "I don't do enough" or "I have to prove myself" or "I'm not good enough" or "I'm not worthy of love" or "I'm unacceptable even to God."

Recovery movements like Alcoholics Anonymous use the acronym HALT to abbreviate some of these feelings. We may experience feelings of hurt (or actual hunger), anger, loneliness, and/or tiredness.

Other ways of describing the hole would be to name the negative feelings as lack, anxiety, shame, anger, guilt, pain, fear, and hurt. The feelings emerging out of our hole can at times seem overwhelming. The hole competes for our attention. I believe that the way we respond to the hole is the critical component in moving toward wholeness.

How we respond either opens us up to deeper expansion in love (wholeness) or restricts our growth by increasing the size and strength of the hole.

The feelings inside the hole scream out for a response. I want to state the obvious: *the only true antidote to human brokenness and anxiety is God's grace.* The hole will go quiet in those moments when we experience the depth of God's love and grace. Tillich writes of such moments:

Grace strikes us when we are in great pain and restlessness. It strikes us when we walk through the dark valley of a meaningless and empty life. It strikes us when we feel that our separation is deeper than usual, because we have violated another life, a life which we loved, or from which we were estranged. It strikes us when our disgust for our own being, our indifference, our weakness, our hostility, and our lack of direction have become intolerable to us. It strikes us when, year after year, the longed-for perfection of life does not appear, when the old compulsions reign within us as they have for decades, when despair destroys all joy and courage. Sometimes at that moment a wave of light breaks into our darkness, and it is as though a voice were saying: "You are accepted, accepted by that which is greater than you, and the name of which you do not know. Do not try to do anything now; perhaps later you will do much. Do not seek for anything, do not perform anything, do not intend anything. Simply accept the fact that you are accepted! If that happens to us, we experience grace."[32]

Tillich writes as one who has felt the sense of lack, fear, guilt, and shame that we suffer as humans. All of us struggle in varying degrees under these forces. The profound danger of these feelings is that they invite us to respond with disordered desires.

The unholy trinity of shame ("I'm not enough"), guilt ("I don't do enough"), and fear ("I don't have enough") intensify our feelings of lack and our desire to mask our pain. The danger is this: desire can only be fully satisfied outside of our abili-

---

32   Paul Tillich, *The Shaking of the Foundations*, repr. ed. (Eugene, OR: Wipf & Stock, 2012), 161–62.

ties and actions. Only God's love will truly fulfill our deepest needs. Grace alone is sufficient. The lie is that our flesh defaults to false solutions. Disordered desires to numb our sense of lack cry out like a siren to a lonely sailor. Aristotle observed, "It is the nature of desire not to be satisfied, and most human beings live only for the gratification of it."[33] All forms of addiction arise from attempts to numb our pain apart from opening fully to God's love and grace through surrender.

Ironically, as soon as we seemingly numb our lack, it returns. Often it shows up even stronger. This reality brings to mind Jesus' reflection in Luke 11:24–26, where he speaks of an unclean spirit who has departed a person. After wandering for a time, it returns to the seemingly clean house, but now it brings seven additional and more evil spirits to live there. Now the person is even worse off than before.

A deep dive spirituality is one committed to opening ourselves to God's grace as a means of growing more fully into the men and women God created us to be. We experience true wholeness only when we shift focus on the hole through the embrace of a way of life that recognizes our nagging sense of lack and the presence of guilt, shame, and fear for what they truly are—signals that we desperately need God's grace and that we cannot fix ourselves with any numbing tactics. We move from the "hole" to *becoming* whole by embracing the means of grace that God has kindly supplied.

What are these means of grace? Wesley wrote, "The chief of these means are prayer, whether in secret or with the great

---

33   Quoted by Gerald May in *Addiction and Grace: Love and Spirituality in the Healing of Addictions* (New York: HarperCollins, 1988), 21.

congregation; searching the Scriptures (which implies reading, hearing, and meditating thereon) and receiving the Lord's Supper, eating bread and drinking wine in remembrance of him; and these we believe to be ordained of God as the ordinary channels of conveying his grace to the souls of men."[34]

Clearly it is vital for us as Christians to pray and to celebrate the Lord's Supper together. These are critical channels of grace and can push back against the hole. These means of grace deserve their own treatment. Our attention in this study focuses on the role that Scripture plays in our transformation and growth in love.

The power of reading Scripture is that it can draw us away from the hole and move us toward true w(hole)ness by breaking up the hardened ground inside of us so that we may receive openhanded the transforming grace of God. But we have to embrace Scripture as a means of grace and make sure that we don't misuse it as a justification for remaining unchanged.

Scripture can be misused or at least functionally ignored because we can easily be distracted. Scripture can be self-justifying instead of self-revealing. We have to resist the temptation to sanitize it lest it lose its power.

The challenge is that our core instinct as men and women is to numb ourselves. The most obvious ways of numbing in the modern world are through alcohol, illegal drugs, prescription drugs, overeating, and sex. These categories gain the most attention because of the destructive addiction patterns that swirl around them.

---

34 John Wesley, *The Sermons of John Wesley: A Collection for the Christian Journey*, ed. Kenneth J. Collins and Jason E. Vickers (Nashville: Abingdon, 2013), 73–74.

The danger for those who don't explicitly struggle in these areas is the temptation to believe that we don't have our own numbing techniques. The truth is that the feelings of lack from our hole also tempt us to numb with more acceptable but nonetheless just as destructive ways. For example, we can easily add addictions to food, social media, video games, exercise, biohacking, and binge-watching TV to the list above.

There is also the most acceptable of all addictions: workaholism. Our culture celebrates overwork. In my experience, the Church does too. Pastors and spiritual leaders often feel compelled to please others and care for everyone except for themselves. So, they work long hours and struggle to take rest. The work we do for God can easily begin to block the work God desires to do in us.

The deeper truth is that many of us cover up our anxiety, guilt, and shame by staying as busy as possible. The problem with more acceptable forms of numbing our pain is that we do not always see immediate negative consequences. The harm is that we slowly calcify and unconsciously block the work of God in our lives.

Growing in grace happens when we recognize our inner turmoil and surrender the pain to God. One of my mentors, Bob Tuttle, taught me the importance of recognizing and creating what he called "low pressure" areas in which the Holy Spirit could work in our lives. What did he mean by "low pressure areas"? He was suggesting that God works most easily in conditions most conducive to our openness to God's grace. Much of this turns on our self-awareness of our ongoing need for God's grace. The hole invites us to a life of distraction, but the Spirit invites us to a larger life of ongoing growth in grace. This bigger future will always involve an increased capacity for loving God, others, and self.

In fact, those who face their addictions often open themselves up more readily to greater levels and depths of God's love for them. This is one of the ironies of the spiritual life. It often takes a serious acknowledgment of our inner darkness before we can find ourselves fully open to God's light.

Luke records a powerful illustration of love at work in Luke 7:36–50. Jesus was dining with a Pharisee named Simon. A woman interrupted the dinner party and approached Jesus. The narrator describes her as a "sinner" (7:37). She stood behind Jesus. This posture was one of deep humility. She could not even face him. Instead, she wept and used her tears to wash Jesus' feet and dry them with her hair. Moreover, she brought a jar of ointment and anointed his feet.

Simon responded to this act of service with indignation that Jesus would let a "sinner" touch him. Jesus shifted the conversation to the topic of the forgiveness of debts. He asked Simon, "Who would love his creditor more? One who was forgiven a vast debt, or one forgiven a smaller one?" Simon of course affirmed that it would be the one who was forgiven much.

Jesus then returned to observing the actions of the woman who had given him an extravagant level of service in contrast to the comparatively meager reception given to him by Simon. Jesus then said, "Therefore I tell you, her sins, which were many, have been forgiven; hence she has shown great love. But the one to whom little is forgiven, loves little" (Luke 7:47).

The truth of the matter is that Simon the Pharisee needed grace just as much as the "sinful" woman. But his spiritual practices made him feel superior to the woman. Ironically, he too was attracted to Jesus. In fact, it was Simon's invitation for Jesus to join him in his home that set the stage for the rich teaching. What is fascinating is that we do not know Simon's response to Jesus' declaration of the woman's forgiveness as well as telling her, "Your faith has saved you; go in peace" (Luke 7:50).

There is no such statement issued to Simon. Did Jesus also forgive him? Did Simon have saving faith as well?

In his important book *Addiction and Grace*, Gerald May describes the deep spirituality of a former addict who one day turns decisively from his or her behavior. He writes of what it is like to experience the hole and turn to God rather than numbing patterns:

A contemplative quality can be found in anyone who has encountered emptiness and chose not to run away. A sense of balance within spaciousness remains within such people, like a window between infinity and the world of everyday experience. They are not only wiser and humbler because of their addictions; they are also more available. Through their spaciousness, they are continually invited homeward. They have in fact, already begun the homeward journey.[35]

I am not making an argument that it is better for each of us to have lived blatantly sinful lives. An abundance of sin is

---

35   Gerald May, *Addiction and Grace*, 160–61.

not a prerequisite for receiving a saving portion of God's grace. As Paul reminded the Romans, "Should we continue in sin in order that grace may abound? By no means!" (Rom 6:1–2). However, Paul is adamant that the Gospel breaks the power of sin in our lives through grace and that God's love grows and multiples in us.

The warning of Jesus' interaction with Simon the Pharisee and the unnamed woman is that we need to avoid the assumptions of Simon. After all, a Pharisee needs grace just as much as a sinner. A few chapters later in Luke, there is another scene involving a Pharisee and a "sinner" (18:9–14). This time it occurs in the temple and the sinner is a man who serves as a tax collector. The Pharisee gave thanks that he was "not like other people: thieves, rogues, adulterers, or even like this tax collector." Instead, he boasted of his religious practices: fasting and tithing.

In contrast, the tax collector simply prayed, "God, be merciful to me, a sinner!" Jesus remarked that the tax collector and not the Pharisee went home justified that day. The tax collector's response would become the core of the Jesus Prayer: "Lord Jesus Christ, Son of God, have mercy on me a sinner."

The subtle temptation is to cover up our lack with external religion. It is one of the great dangers for us as followers of Jesus. We can substitute God-talk for a moment-by-moment relationship with the living God. What do I mean?

God-talk is when we describe and discuss God in the third person. It's when we focus on facts and details without going deeper and asking about the implications for how we live our lives. It's making the mistake of substituting information about the Gospel for the transformational promises of the Gospel. It's mistaking mastery of the content of Scripture for Scripture's mastery of our hearts.

When we read about Jesus' encounters with the Pharisees, it is easy to pass judgment on these persons. They come off as judgmental, prudish, and masters of missing the point.

In Matthew 23:25–28, Jesus says to them:

> "Woe to you, scribes and Pharisees, hypocrites! For you clean the outside of the cup and of the plate, but inside they are full of greed and self-indulgence. You blind Pharisee! First clean the inside of the cup, so that the outside also may become clean."

> "Woe to you, scribes and Pharisees, hypocrites! For you are like whitewashed tombs, which on the outside look beautiful, but inside they are full of the bones of the dead and of all kinds of filth. So you also on the outside look righteous to others, but inside you are full of hypocrisy and lawlessness."

Who exactly were these seemingly clueless Pharisees? One of the surprising truths I discovered early in my theological education is that the Pharisees were almost universally admired by the people of Jesus' day. The Pharisees were reformers. They loved the Scriptures and sought to live them out faithfully in their day. They believed that the future of God's people depended on their personal holiness. They had a mission to teach the people to live faithfully and avoid the corruptions of the world. They vigorously desired to apply the Scriptures to their world.

Sounds familiar, right? Most of us who love the Bible and seek to live faithfully in our day as followers of Jesus understand our mission of evangelism and justice in similar ways. The problem with the Pharisees is that they ended up loving their interpretations of Scripture more than the deeper truth of Scripture about Jesus and the kingdom. They viewed Jesus as a threat because Jesus didn't follow their rules.

One of Jesus' most famous rebukes was when a group of Pharisees criticized Jesus for eating with tax collectors and sinners. Jesus had just called Matthew the tax collector into his band of disciples. Jesus recognized the opportunity to reach more of Matthew's associates. These were the persons whom the Pharisees labeled "sinners," that is, persons on the outside of the faith. How did Jesus defend his actions? He quoted Scripture and added a clear implication of its truth: "Go and learn what this means, 'I desire mercy, not sacrifice.' For I have come to call not the righteous but sinners" (Matt 9:13 cf. Hos 6:6).

The Pharisees covered up their lack with multiple coats of religious legalism. They chose rules over a deep relationship grounded in the love of God, neighbor, and self.

Now let me be clear: I'm not suggesting that following Jesus involves an "anything goes" lifestyle. It is certainly critical and necessary to ask, "How shall we live then in light of the good news?" Or "What does it mean to live as a follower of Jesus today?" There are habits and practices that do in fact enhance our witness and help us grow in grace. We simply must stay on guard against the subtle temptation of a judgmental legalism that gives us *certainty* in an uncertain world.

Remember Jesus' powerful teaching to his disciples about the Pharisees. Jesus didn't come to erase the Law. He came to fulfill it. In fact, he warned, "Unless your righteousness exceeds that of the scribes and Pharisees, you will never enter the kingdom of heaven" (Matt 5:20). Strong words. If we think of the Pharisees as misguided zealots, we miss the power of Jesus' teaching. Imagine believing (as many of Jesus' hearers would have) that the scribes and Pharisees were the exemplars of righteous and then hearing Jesus say that their high standards were not radical enough.

What would an even higher standard look like? Jesus describes it in terms of perfection in love. True wholeness is the fulfillment of the commands to love God and to love neighbor as we love ourselves. Matthew 5:48 reads, "Be perfect, therefore, as your heavenly Father is perfect." Most of us recoil from Jesus' command and look for an interpretation that softens a clear command. However, many in the early Church believed Jesus was serious.[36] What if he was?

What would it look like to grow in ever-increasing love for God, neighbor, and self? What if the purpose of our existence was to expand more in love?

Yes, I am speaking about a certain level of mystery and uncertainty. When Jesus offers us the heavenly Father as the model for love, our minds can easily move to the impossibilities for us as finite beings to grasp the infinite.

---

36   Bondi, *To Love as God Loves,* 17 (see chap. 9, n. 3).

Jesus offers us a pathway forward through two images. First, in Matthew 5:43–47, Jesus describes the fullest expression of love as one that is *indiscriminate*. The illustrations for this are God causing the sun to rise on both the good and the bad and God sending rain on both the just and the unjust. In other words, God's love is not inhibited by a set of rules that declares outsiders to be unworthy of love or redefines "neighbor" to mean only persons who love us in return.

The Pharisees were genuine in their zeal. But in their quest for righteousness, they exchanged the certainty of their self-serving interpretations for the mystery of God's infinite capacity for love. In a conversation with Dr. Gerrardo Martí on my podcast, he talked about the danger of seeing the world through our limited perspectives that he learned from a mentor. It goes this way, "My game, my rules, my field, my ball, I win."[37] Our desire for control even in our quest for growth in grace can throttle the deep work that God desires to do in our lives. We may win the game that we think we are supposed to be playing only to discover that God was calling us to a bigger life in an infinite game.

The Pharisees substituted their system of self-sanctification for the Spirit-driven sanctification that God alone offers. What does this have to do with the struggle for w(hole)ness?

If we want to experience true wholeness, we must resist the impulse to embrace forms of religion that provide a quick fix to the anxiety of the hole. The Pharisees found certainty at the cost of missing the Messiah.

37 Brian Russell, *The Deep Dive Spirituality Conversations Podcast*, "Episode 10: Religion, Class, and the Racial Divide with Dr. Gerardo Marti," June 4, 2020, https://deepdivespirituality.podbean.com/e/episode-10-religion-class-and-the-racial-divide-with-dr-gerardo-marti/.

What price would you pay for a false certainty? Let go of the need for a neat and tidy faith. Deep down we know that there's way more to God than our easy cliché answers. I am not suggesting the embrace of heterodox positions. But I am suggesting that we let go of our need for control. Instead let us welcome the full implications of the Bible into our lives—especially those passages that make us uncomfortable.

Our commitment to the authority of Scripture turns on our willingness to submit to the texts that offend us the most. It's easy to follow and advocate for the Bible's teaching when it impinges on the lives of others. The true test of faithfulness occurs when we hear the Word calling us to change. It is only when we have true "skin in the game" that we can explore our own contradictions and open ourselves anew to a deep cleansing.

In the next chapter, we'll explore the idea of becoming the first convert to any part of the Bible we are listening to or studying.

Questions for Reflection

- What does "w(hole)ness" mean to you?

- What means do you use to cover up your hole, that is, feelings of discomfort caused by guilt, shame, fear, and anxiety?

- How do the Pharisees illustrate how our religious commitments can actually run counter to the deep work God desires to do in us and in the lives of others?

Chapter Eleven:
Interpretation as Conversion

Long ago, I recognized that the primary purpose of reading the Bible is *conversion*.[38] I'm talking about my own conversion first and then the conversion of others to whom I have the privilege of teaching, preaching, or sharing the Gospel. If I haven't personally been converted to the message of the text, I risk playing the Pharisee and imposing on others ideals and standards that I myself don't follow.

What does it mean to convert to the message of the text? It means listening to Scripture for what it demands of my life and then realigning myself with it. It involves praying for deep astonishment and illumination, so that I can be sensitive to my blind spots and glaring areas of hypocrisy. It involves risking being open to surprise attacks from the text on our present sense of holiness.

---

38 See my *(Re)Aligning with God: Reading Scripture for Church and World* (Eugene, OR: Cascade, 2016) for a book-length treatment of this idea from the perspective of a missional hermeneutic. In fact, the first sentence of chapter 1 reads, "The goal of biblical interpretation is conversion," 1.

John Wesley wrote a powerful sermon, "The Repentance of Believers," in which he recognized our need for repentance subsequent to our justification and new birth.[39] Wesley saw this second act of repentance as a critical doorway to the deeper transformation that he called entire sanctification or Christian perfection. Wesley in particular zeroed in on feelings of pride or superiority, self-will, jealousy, unkind speech, sins of omission, and inward defects. Of inward defects, it is notable that Wesley spoke of lingering guilt, fear, and struggles loving God.[40]

Wesley appears to be talking about the lingering effects of the *hole* in our movement to wholeness. Our love becomes distorted by the unholy trinity of guilt ("I don't do enough"), shame ("I'm not enough"), and fear ("I don't have enough"). Wesley reads these feelings as signals that point to the need for sanctifying grace.

The good news is that God's grace is abundant and able to transform us. Sanctifying grace slowly saturates us so that we reflect more consistently the values of the kingdom, such as the fruits of the spirit: love, joy, peace, patience, kindness, generosity, faithfulness, gentleness, and self-control. These virtues are ways of describing a life that grows in love for God, neighbor, and self.

The problem is the allure of the false promises of the flesh. Our flesh longs for relief from fear, guilt, and shame. The constant temptation is to soothe our lostness with human solutions such as religious legalism or commitments to grand causes. Confronting our inner pain and guilt is hard.

---

39 Wesley, *The Sermons of John Wesley,* 569–80 (see chap. 10, n. 3).

40 Wesley Sermons, 575, esp. paragraphs 15–16.

Jesus' profound question, "For what will it profit them if they gain the whole world but forfeit their life?" (Matt 16:26) comes to mind. When we face the pain of the hole and refuse to soothe it with false solutions, we are ready for transformation.

I'm willing to approach Scripture from a position of being somewhere between an uncertain certainty and a certain uncertainty. I am willing to feel the pain and ache of anxiety and the sense of lack because I know that there is a deeper magic to be found by not succumbing to the world's siren song of easy comfort. I'm willing to risk the temporary discomfort of inner transformation for the possibility of a long-term deep-dive spirituality. Scripture shows us the way if we are willing to take a plunge into its depths.

When we read Scripture, we will hear its call for ongoing repentance. Jesus opened his public ministry with a powerful exhortation to a total realignment of life and priorities: "Repent, for the kingdom of heaven is at hand" (Matt 4:17 NIV; cf. Mark 1:15). A better translation is, "Be continually repenting, for the kingdom of heaven is at hand." Jesus does not have a onetime act in mind. Moreover, the power of Jesus' call to ongoing repentance is in its comprehensiveness. Jesus does not qualify or limit the scope by providing any specific guidance. There is no wiggle room. There is no checklist. Jesus is calling us to rid ourselves of anything that hinders us from fully embodying the kingdom.

The only clue as to how to repent is found in Jesus' next action. He calls disciples to participate in God's mission by *following* him (Matt 4:18–22). In other words, Jesus' life

122 | **Astonished by the Word** | Brian D. Russell

and teaching serve as the litmus test for our repentance.
Repentance becomes a way of life rather than a mile marker
we reach. As we follow Jesus into the world on mission, we
continually realign ourselves as we navigate the path. The
way of Jesus is not static. The only way to follow Jesus is
to be in constant motion. But whenever we are moving,
we have to make small and sometimes large adjustments to
maintain our course. These adjustments are what repentance
looks like.

How do we know what adjustments to make? This is where
Scripture helps us. The Jesus whom we follow is the Jesus revealed in Scripture. To simply ask, "What would Jesus do?" is
insufficient apart from a habitual engagement with the Bible.
Apart from Scripture's witness, we will create a Jesus who essentially mirrors our values. To make Jesus in our image is to
practice idolatry. Ironic, isn't it?

How do we avoid making Jesus in our image? It's committing to being the first convert to whatever part of Scripture we
are reading. It's always recognizing how the text challenges us
before pondering all the ways that this text calls into question
the lives and beliefs of others. It's being mindful of Jesus' warning to the scribes and Pharisees who were seeking to stone a
woman caught in adultery. They sought to draw Jesus into a
trap, but he wisely replied to them, "Let anyone among you
who is without sin be the first to throw a stone against her"
(John 8:7). Jesus was not excusing the woman's sin. Instead,
Jesus models a restorative approach. He was without sin (and
could have picked up a stone and thrown it with integrity). Yet
he did not condemn her. Rather he sent her home with the

exhortation, "Go your way, and from now on do not sin again" (John 8:11).[41]

What is the key bulwark against idolatry? It's Scripture. The entire point of this book is to advocate a reading of the Bible that calls us to ongoing transformation in such a way that allows us to impact the world. Jesus' call to his disciples in Matthew 4:18–22 was *missional, communal,* and *transformational.* It was missional because Jesus called the disciples to become persons who would "fish for people." It was *communal* because Jesus calls a group and not merely individuals. Matthew 4:18–22 records Jesus calling two sets of brothers, so there was never a moment when there wasn't a community. It was *transformational* in the sense that by following Jesus the disciples were committed to becoming like their master.

In his letter, James warns against hearing the word apart from doing. Reading Scripture for deep formation involves hearing *and* doing. The proof is in the actions that we take in aligning ourselves with the message of the Scripture. To remain the same according to James is to be like "those who look at themselves in a mirror . . . and, on going away, immediately forget what they were like." I trust that none reading these words desires to forget his or her reflection.

In the next chapter, we'll explore the Shema or Great Commandment for how its vision of full devotion deepens our commitment to idolatherapy as a means for growth in love for God, neighbor, and self.

---

41 John 7:53–8:11 is not found in the earliest known copies of John's Gospel. It however is fully in line with what we know of the character of Jesus. For a rich discussion of the textual issues and an openness to the historical reliability of this account, see George R. Beasley-Murray, *John* (Waco, TX: Word Biblical Commentaries, 1987), 143–47.

Questions for Reflection

- Where do I struggle to align or realign my life with the message of Jesus?

- What are the blind spots in which I'm not the first convert to the texts that I study?

- Where do I need to be reminded to put into action the clear teaching of Scripture?

- What is really holding me back from living out the Word?

Chapter Twelve:
The Shema as a Guide for Living the Word

One of the core confessions in Scripture is the Shema, or Great Commandment:[42]

Hear, O Israel: The lord is our God, the lord alone. You shall love the lord your God with all your heart, and with all your soul, and with all your might. (Deut 6:4–5)

Verse 4 begins with the exhortation: "Hear." The first step when approaching Scripture is embracing its call to receive the Word. To hear is to listen and take action. There is no true hearing without a faithful response. I call this having "skin in the game." Scripture needs to be embodied in our minds, bodies, and outward actions.

The remainder of verse 4 may be translated several different ways. For example, the above translation follows the

---

42 Elements of this chapter first appeared in Brian D. Russell, "Conversations with Scripture (4): Idolatry," Catalyst, April 24, 2017, http://www.cata-lystresources.org/conversations-with-scripture-4-idolatry/.

NRSV.[43] The ESV, NKJV, and NIV (among others) read, "The lord is our God, the Lord is One." The challenge for translators and interpreters is how best to understand the Hebrew word *'echad*. Its basic meaning is "one." But what does "one" mean in this context? Is it a focus on the uniqueness and unity of the Lord?[44] Or is it emphasizing the singular exclusive commitment of God's people to the Lord as *their* God? The English translations shared above highlight these dimensions.

Old Testament scholar Walter Moberly has suggested a pathway through this dilemma. He suggests that the idea may be expressed by thinking of the Lord as Israel's "one and only."[45] The same word translated "one" in Deuteronomy 6:4 is also found in Song of Songs 6:8–9:

There are sixty queens and eighty concubines,

and maidens without number.

My dove, my perfect one, is the only one,

the darling of her mother,

flawless to her that bore her.

The maidens saw her and called her happy;

the queens and concubines also, and they praised her.

The emphasis in the Song of Songs was on the selection of the beloved out of all competing options available for the writer. His

43   The CEB is similar, with "Our God is the Lord! Only the Lord."

44   See S. Dean McBride Jr. "The Yoke of the Kingdom: An Exposition of Deuteronomy 6:4" *Interpretation* 27, no. 3 (1973): 273–306.

45   R. W. L. Moberly, *Old Testament Theology*, 7–40 (see chap. 8, n. 2).

choice of his wife involved recognizing her incomparable uniqueness as well as the reality that there were innumerable other options available. Yet, the author chose his beloved as his "one and only."

The issue at stake in Deuteronomy as well as in our world today is twofold. First, there were competing gods in the Near East, and as we discussed earlier, there are myriads of "gods" competing for our commitment today. At minimum, Deuteronomy 6:4–5 calls for absolute allegiance to the Lord. Israel and we who seek to follow Jesus today are to choose the Lord for exclusive service over all others. Second, the God of Scripture is incomparable to any other deity. God's incomparability is the reason for Scripture's adamant opposition to idolatry in any form. God is unique as Israel's "one and only." Other powers, ideologies, commitments, and philosophies of life can and do take on the form of gods and demand religious zeal from their followers. However, if the incomparable God of Scripture is indeed God, there cannot be any other god for God's people (cf. Deut 4:35, 39). Moreover, it is then a falsehood to even use the word "god" for any other being outside of the Lord.[46] Yes there are other entities that compete for our allegiance, but if the Lord is indeed the transcendent God of creation, then it is inappropriate to call any of these competing entities "god." The Lord is qualitatively different and thus must be embraced exclusively by God's people. Then we can order our lives in faithful obedience to King Jesus as the rest of Deuteronomy 6:5–9 lays out.

How do we respond to the Lord as our "one and only"? Verse 5 demands a response of a radical and devoted love. Faithful commit-

---

46   See Christopher Wright, *Mission of God: Unlocking the Bible's Grand Narrative* (Westmont, IL: InterVarsity Press, 2006), 136–88.

ment rather than sentimentalism captures the meaning of the love envisioned. This is not to deny an emotional response to God. Love is a feeling in our bodies and a reality to express consciously. Verse 5 calls for a moment-by-moment decision to embody faithfulness. The phrases "with all your heart, and with all your soul, and with all your might" form a triad emphasizing our whole-person response to God. "Heart" refers to the will or thinking center of a person. "all your soul" often is misunderstood as the spiritual part of a person. It is actually bigger than this. In fact, *soul* here refers to all aspects of us as a living being. So, "All your might" becomes a magnifier that emphatically restates the need for a full commitment. We may better translate the phrase as "with all of your best intentions and decisions, and with all that you are as a man or woman, and with everything else you can muster." Together this triad calls for an "all in" response by us to the Lord as our "one and only."

Is the Lord truly our "one and only"? What would it look like if we de-elevated all other gods and lifted up King Jesus? Is this not the heart of the confession "Jesus is Lord"? This is a conversation that Scripture desires to have with us. We explored the impediments in the preceding chapters.

How do we live out our commitment to King Jesus as our "one and only"? Deuteronomy 6:6–9 is a critical text for reflecting on how Scripture may work in our lives:

Keep these words that I am commanding you today in your heart. Recite them to your children and talk about them when you are at home and when you are away, when you lie down and when you rise. Bind them as a sign on your hand, fix them as an emblem on your forehead, and write them on the doorposts of your house and on your gates.

The first word, *keep,* is slightly misleading. The Hebrew word is actually the "to be" verb. A better translation is, "These words that I am commanding you today will be in your heart." Living out the Great Commandment is inseparable from abiding in the Word.

It is easy to be distracted by verses 7–9, which focus on the habits of teaching and external performance. But before we can share the words with others, they must have their way with us. They must become the subject of our lives and not merely the object of our focus.

Part of the application of the Great Commandment in Deuteronomy 6:6–9 is on creating an intergenerational community of faith. The grace that we receive must be passed on to others. But we must receive and live it first. The word is to be in our hearts. As we learned above, heart is not the emotional core of a person. It is the center of our thinking, intention setting, and decision-making.

Similar to the inside-out movement of the Great Commandment, 6:6–9 imagines the words of the Lord through Moses reaching us in our hearts. It then moves to our family as we are charged with teaching them to our children. Then verses 7–9 include more public declarations of the Word through visible signs to ourselves, and to others.

Faithful Scripture-centered living involves skin in the game. It is not enough to pass on the Bible's teachings to others if they have not first deeply penetrated our hearts. The teaching ministry of the Christ-following movement stands and falls on the transformation of those who teach and preach. The challenge is that it is easier to measure knowledge than it is to measure transformation. Yet, obedience is less an intellectual problem than it is a heart and hands problem. We've all seen this challenge in others. If we are discerning, we can recognize this truth in our lives as well. Filling our minds with the right doctrine and the ability to pass an objective test on the contents of Scripture is not a guarantee of a heart and body that will reflect God's holy love in the world.

In Deuteronomy, Moses rejects making the faith a mere intellectual pursuit. Getting the word in our hearts first is a critical move. It means that the core of our being is aligned with God's will. Then we share it with others as a commitment to live out before a watching world.

Contrast the dynamic vision of Deuteronomy 6:6–9 with the typical way that we teach. In the West, we often tend to value experts who can explain the details of a passage over a faithful and ordinary Christian. The result is the loss of esteem for the teaching office of local pastors as well as for faithful laity who tangibly model love for God and neighbor in their local contexts on a daily basis.

Instead, we are tempted to prize the work of experts and even celebrity speakers. Theology becomes an objective description of God or even of discipleship. Of course, there is a place for faithful objective teaching, but it must be done in tandem with clear modeling and practical tools for implementation. Otherwise, we run into what Peter Rollins describes in *The Fidelity of Betrayal*. Rollins writes, "In this way Christianity is given over to the scholar who sits at her desk, surrounded on all sides by an endless sea of ink, adding her own tiny drops so as to justify her living. The truth of Christianity is thus given over to those who can dissect it, study it, and reflect upon it."[47] I'm not denying the importance of good scholarship. But we must not lose sight of the fact that faithful scholarship must be the servant of deep transformation and not an end in itself. I've learned much from reading and studying the Bible and theology at the highest level, but when I look back at my life, I am most grateful for the men and women who modeled what a transformed life looks like and loved me enough to teach me the way of Jesus.

The New Testament assumes that faithful doctrine is taught by people who live it out both publicly and privately. Jesus modeled this practice during his earthly ministry. When he called his first disciples, he said, "Follow me, and I will make you fish for people" (Matt 4:19). The focus for the disciples was Jesus: his teaching and way of living. In Matthew 5:1–9:38, he taught and lived out the kingdom message that he preached. By following Jesus, the disciples caught the core of the Gospel as much as they were taught it. The apostles modeled it no less confidently than Jesus. Consider Paul's audacious exhortation in Philippians 3:17, "Brothers and sisters, join in imitating me, and observe those who live according to the example you have in us." The "us" includes Paul's coworkers in Philippi, Timothy and Epaphroditus (2:19–30). In essence, Paul is saying: Live your life after my example as well as after the example of Timothy and Epaphroditus.

---

47   Peter Rollins, *The Fidelity of Betrayal: Towards a Church Beyond Belief* (Brewster, MA: Paraclete Press, 2008), 92.

The endgame of idolatherapy as we have described it in part 2 is a transformed life that leads to even greater love for God and neighbor. It begins with opening ourselves to transformation so that the Word can penetrate into every part of our being. In part 3, we will focus on how to implement the ideas of this book and give examples of reading Scripture for deep transformation in the love of God and neighbor.

Questions for Reflection

- What does it mean for God to be your "one and only"?

- What is more important according to Deuteronomy 6:4–9: right doctrine or right living?

- Who are some of the faithful Christians who have modeled for you the way of Jesus?

Part Three:
Drinking from the Well

Chapter Thirteen:
Contemplative Reading—Strategies for Preparing the Heart for Even More of God

The Bible isn't a magical book. It doesn't yield its riches by praying a certain prayer or using a particular interpretive method. I want to return to Barth's idea of Scripture "becoming the word of God" that we discussed in chapter 1. Deep formation occurs through the work of the Holy Spirit illuminating the text that we are reading. Transformational reading involves a synergy between us and God. So how can we consistently experience a Holy Spirit–led encounter with the Bible that calls us to a deeper level of love for God and neighbor?

In this chapter, you'll gain new insights on creating the proper set and setting for the study of Scripture. I'll share ways to integrate contemplative spiritual practices before and during your study time. You'll create a plan of implementation that works for your specific needs.

Set: Be Clear on Your Goal and Purpose

Before reading Scripture, be clear about your goal and purpose. In the next chapter, I'll share some additional information on mindsets and questions that you can bring to your study. You may be wondering why I'm spending time on what may appear to be obvious. Don't we read the Bible to draw closer to God and be transformed? The answer is: "Of Course!" But then why do we find ourselves often in ruts or dry times? Why does reading the Bible sometimes feel like "going through the motions" or something that we *should* do?

Let's be honest. Much Bible reading occurs because we believe that it's part of being a Christian. It simply becomes a habit. Or as pastors, we are paid to read Scripture so that we can preach and teach our congregations. Sometimes we read Scripture transactionally—we look for a nugget of wisdom for the day and then move on to our work. Or we read only to discover content for our next sermon or lesson or blog post. Sometimes we pick up the Bible out of muscle memory and quickly skim through its familiar pages without digging any deeper than our last pass through the text.

If you resonate at all with the preceding paragraph, then what I'm about to share about set or intention will be valuable. Make it your intention to be transformed by most of your work with Scripture. It's not presumptuous to state your purpose. I believe that God honors clear intentions and focus.

Let's go back to Augustine's advice again: "So anyone who thinks that he has understood the divine scriptures or any part of them but cannot by his understanding build up this double love of God and neighbor has not yet succeeded in understanding them."[48]

Setting: Create a Ceremony or Ritual Around Your Work with the Bible

If our intention is a deep transformational reading of the Word, we need to create containers for the experience. If I try to read Scripture in a loud and noisy public setting, I may find myself too distracted to focus. If my sole engagement with the text is via audio during my daily commute to work or errands or during a workout, I may zone out of listening from time to time. So if I gain an insight, I may not have the opportunity to capture it. If I read Scripture surrounded by commentaries and study aids, I may end up focusing more on what others have said about the Word rather than pondering it deeply on its own terms before interacting with the insights of others.

Also, it is difficult to read the Bible wisely and well when we are fatigued or overstressed or anxious. I'm not suggesting that we only read the Bible when conditions are ideal. Instead, I'm naming situations that challenge our study. If we create rituals or ceremonies around our work with Scripture, we can mitigate some of the external forces. We will also create spaces for confronting the inner forces that block the work of the Spirit in our lives as we discussed in part 2.

48 Augustine, *On Christian Teaching,* 27 (see intro., n. 1).

Brief Guide to a Ritual for Transformational *Lectio Divina*

There are four movements in *lectio divina*. *Lectio divina* is a Latin phrase that means "divine reading." It can be used as a method in and of itself, but I view it as a container for intentional contemplative engagement with God via the Bible. If you are trained in formal exegetical or inductive Bible study methods, you don't have to stop using those resources. Also, you can read the text in Greek or Hebrew (if you are able) and still practice lectio divina. I recommend a contemplative approach to the Bible, because fundamentally, reading Scripture is about *our conversion* to the text as a means of growing deeper in our love for God and neighbor.

Set aside time for your study of the Word. Allow at least 30 minutes for a session, but for deep study consider spending even longer. You can combine multiple sessions together if you are preparing teaching or preaching materials on a text. I personally recommend setting aside 60- or 90-minute blocks for intentional study. I'm including the time we will be spending preparing our hearts before opening the Bible and then processing our findings at the end.

Preparation: Silent Meditative Prayer and/or Spiritual Journaling (5–20 minutes)

I've found it critical to prepare my soul for the Word. Just as we need to stretch and warm up before exercising or playing a sport, we need a "pregame" ritual to prepare us for intentional study. In part 2 we focused on the idea of *idolatherapy* as a means of confronting those inner forces that seek to deform us and set up blocks to the deep work God desires to do in us. I highly recommend experimenting with contemplative spiritual habits as a means of unblocking our inner spiritual plumbing.

Centering Prayer or Silent Meditative Prayer

Silent prayer can help prepare our hearts and minds for what God has for us.[49] I'm not talking about praying with words but literally *wordless* prayer. Centering prayer involves sitting quietly in God's presence and surrendering the thoughts, feelings, images, and tapes that play in our minds. This ancient practice has its roots in the desert fathers and mothers. They found it helpful for the ongoing process of transformation. Silent meditative prayer is a powerful means of deepening our love for God and neighbor through the practice of conscious surrender of our inner world to God.

Here are steps for incorporating a session of centering prayer into your Bible study ritual:

(1) Choose a prayer word. You will use this word to recenter on your intention to surrender your inner world and sit in silence with the God who loves you. I personally use and recommend the word *Jesus*. But you can use any short word of two to three syllables that serves as a means of gently letting go of whatever has captured your attention.

(2) Set a timer on your watch or phone for 5–20 minutes. Of course, you can go longer if you desire.

---

49 See my *Centering Prayer: Sitting Quietly in God's Presence Can Change Your Life* (Brewster, MA: Paraclete Press, 2021) for a full discussion.

(3) Start the timer, close your eyes, and pray: "Lord, Jesus Christ, Son of God, have mercy on me." or "Here I am, Lord. Speak, for your servant is listening."

(4) Whenever you notice that you are lost in a thought, memory, or feeling, gently return to the silence by uttering your prayer word and recentering. Do not be frustrated if you find yourself constantly distracted and lost in thoughts. It is how our minds work. The idea of the time in silence is to allow our minds to settle as a means of preparing for intimate fellowship with God. If you are new to centering prayer, you will likely be amazed at how busy your mind is. Centering prayer is a means of living out Paul's exhortation to "take every thought captive to obey Christ" (2 Cor 10:5).

You may find it helpful to remember the Four Rs of Centering Prayer:[50]

(1) Resist no thought. Our minds create thoughts incessantly, so don't fight them.

(2) Retain no thought. Simply allow the thoughts to flow without giving your attention to them. This means letting go of all thoughts whether they be profound, mundane, or troubling.

(3) React to no thought. Do not judge your thoughts. You may encounter ones rooted in Evagrius's eight

---

50 Cynthia Bourgeault, *The Heart of Centering Prayer: Nondual Christianity in Theory and Practice* (Boulder, CO: Shambala, 2016), 32.

evil thoughts. You may feel guilt, shame, or fear. Learn to be nonreactive to them.

(4) Return gently to Jesus with your sacred word. When a thought captures your attention or you become reactive to it, simply and gently deploy your prayer word as a means of releasing it. Think of this step as handing your thoughts to God. The beauty of this transaction is it involves *surrender*. As we surrender our thoughts, whether they be profound, mundane, or troubling, God will slowly do the work of breaking up the hardened soil within to prepare us for the good seeds of Scripture to be planted.

When the timer goes off, take a few breaths, and then offer a regular Prayer to God. I'll use prayers from the Book of Common prayer or simply utter one extemporaneously.

Spiritual Journaling

As a final step before moving to engage the Scriptures in lectio divina, experiment with spending 3–5 minutes answering these two questions:

(1) What are 3–5 people, things, or events that I can be grateful for today? Gratitude is another way to prime your soul for deep work with Scripture. Gratitude is one of those feelings and inner dispositions that can change your life over time. Paul exhorted the Colossians, "And whatever you do, in word or deed,

do everything in the name of the Lord Jesus, giving thanks to God the Father through him" (Col 3:17). Cicero wrote, "Gratitude is not only the greatest of the virtues, but the parent of all of the others." Prepare your heart for Scripture by filling it with thanksgiving.

(2) What lingering thoughts, feelings, or sensations seem to be present in my mind or body and bothering me? Do a thought or feeling "download" in your journal. Notice any feeling of unease. Are you angry at someone? Are you disappointed? Do you feel odd sensations in your stomach or stiffness in your neck and shoulders? What may be causing these discomforts? Be brutally honest and get it all on paper. I can promise you that this simple practice will advance your experience of idolatherapy and help to clear blockages for the work that God desires to do in your life today as you read the Word.

Please take seriously these preparatory steps. I've been doing these for almost a decade now, and I'm certain that if you embrace them, you'll see tangible results over time in your spiritual formation. Even more importantly, those persons whom you serve as well as your friends and family will notice the changes in you.

The Steps of Lectio Divina (20–120 minutes)

There are four core steps to lectio divina.[51] *Lectio* (reading the text), *meditatio* (meditating and pondering its message), *oratio* (praising God), and *contemplatio* (contemplating how to live out the text for others).

Think of the first two steps as breathing in the good news and then the last two as breathing out love for God and neighbor. Inspiration and expiration. Inspiration and expiration. Don't be afraid to take conscious breaths in and out during your study. Visualize and even feel the flow of oxygen and energy moving in and out of your body as you ponder the Word deeply. Such a practice will keep you grounded and present and open to what God desires to reveal through your reading of Scripture. Whenever you find yourself distracted as you study, simply return to your breathing and pray a simple prayer: "Jesus, help me" or "Here I am, Lord. Speak to me" or "Astonish me anew" or "Teach me, Lord, for I am listening."

Let's now explore what each step of lectio divina involves. Begin first with a prayer for illumination. Here are some of my favorites from saints from the past. Bede (c. 673–735) was a great scholar in the early English church. He lived as a monk in Jarrow. Here is a prayer that he composed for use when studying the Bible:

---

51 The time suggestions turn on your broader intentions to your study. If you are using lectio for your daily devotional time, you can default to a shorter period of study. If you are preparing a lesson or sermon, you will likely be taking a deeper dive that will require more time. I personally don't recommend going longer than two hours without a break. You can always work through the steps over multiple sessions.

May your Spirit, O Christ, lead me in the right way, keeping me safe from all forces of evil and destruction. And, free from all malice, may I search diligently in your Holy Word to discover with the eyes of my mind your commandments. Finally, give me the strength of will to put those commandments into practice through all the days of my life. Amen.

Gregory of Nazianus (329–89) was one of the key early Church fathers who worked during the pivotal fourth century. Here is a prayer that he wrote for help in interpreting the book of Psalms:

Lord, as I read the Psalms, let me hear you singing. As I read your words, let me hear you speaking. As I reflect on each page, let me see your image. And as I seek to put your precepts into practice, let my heart be filled with joy. Amen.

Origen (c. 185–c. 254), a skilled interpreter and theologian, was one of the greatest early church fathers. Here is a prayer that he composed for use in the study of the Scriptures:

Lord, inspire us to read your Scriptures and meditate upon them day and night. We beg you to give us real understanding of what we need, that we in turn may put its precepts into practice. Yet we know that understanding and good intentions are worthless, unless rooted in your graceful love. So we ask that the words of Scriptures may also be not just signs on a page, but channels of grace into our hearts. Amen.

The last prayer that I will share comes from Thomas Aquinas (c. 1225–74). Aquinas was the most prominent theologian of the medieval period. This prayer was intended for use before Aquinas preached or wrote. I find this one particularly profound:

O Creator of the universe, who has set the stars in the heavens and causes the sun to rise and set, shed the light of your wisdom into the darkness of my mind. Fill my thoughts with the loving knowledge of you, that I may bring your light to others. Just as you can make even babies speak your truth, instruct my tongue and guide my pen to convey the wonderful glory of the Gospel. Make my intellect sharp, my memory clear, and my words eloquent, so that I may faithfully interpret the mysteries which you have revealed. Amen.

Here is my personal prayer for illumination:

Our living and loving God, astonish us anew with the riches of your Word. Astonish me and give me ears to hear all that you desire. Amen.

Lectio Divina: Breathing in the Word

In lectio and meditatio, we breathe in the Word of God and ponder its message.

Lectio (reading). We first begin with reading or listening to the text that we intend to explore in depth. Read through it multiple times in your primary language. If you are an audio learner, listen to a recording of the text. Likewise, if you have ability in Greek or Hebrew, read it in the original. If you are multilingual, read it in the other languages that you speak. The goal here is to experience the text. Ponder the language. Pay attention to flow of the words.

Focus on answering these broad questions:

What is going on in this passage?

What is being emphasized?

Who is being addressed (individuals or a group, the Church, or the world)?

Are there recurring terms or ideas?

If you are familiar with the wider context of the larger book, how does the text you are studying connect with the paragraph or chapter immediately preceding and the one following?

Make notes. It's critical to write down the observations and insights that you are discovering. Remember to stay in a prayerful attitude. If you find yourself distracted, return to your intention of being open to astonishment.

Meditatio (meditate/ponder). In this step, we begin to chew on the specific discoveries we made in lectio. In lectio, the focus was on a careful, slow movement through a smaller passage of Scripture. In meditatio, we expand the scope of our reading. We now metaphorically "chew," or meditate, on our text in light of what we know about the rest of Scripture, theology, and our personal/communal experiences. Moreover, we also set our text within the wider conversation that the Church has previously had with our text. The goal is to focus on integrating the insights we gained in lectio into our previous knowledge as a means of bringing them fully to life in our soul. For suggested resources to help you engage the wider interpretive conversation, see the list at the end of this chapter.

Ask yourself questions such as these:

How does this text confirm, challenge, or expand what I know of other parts of Scripture?

How does this text confirm, challenge, or expand my present understanding of God, Jesus, sin, creation, leadership, ministry, holiness, Christian living, mission, or life together as God's people?

Please observe that the previous question is not an exhaustive list of topics. The key in meditatio is to place your reflection from the lectio stage into dialogue with the knowledge and experiences that you brought to today's study as well as to explore a resource or two to help you understand the interpretations that others have made. Continue to make notes of your observations and insights.

Lectio Divina: Breathing Out the Word

In *oratio* and *contemplatio*, we breathe back out the Word of God as an intentional act of loving God and loving our neighbor. The two steps in the second half of lectio divina involve what is typically called application in Bible Study. We are now ready to reflect intentionally on Augustine's "double love of God and neighbor." The critical shift that we need to make in our study of Scripture is the steadfast refusal to apply the Word to anyone or anything outside of ourselves *until* we have felt the true weight of the Word in our minds, hearts, and souls.

The second half of lectio divina is also critical lest we allow the Word to enter our lives without intentionally taking action on it. As James taught us, we are to be "doers of the word" (1:22). It is better to study and apply one text of Scripture than it is to "know" the content of the entire Bible without living out its precepts, or worse, fooling ourselves into equating a knowledge about God with actually knowing God.

Oratio (praise). The first application focuses on your relationship with God. Based on your breathing in the Word during lectio and meditatio, how does the text want to leave your body as an intentional expression of your love for God? How would you pray back the text to God?

Pay careful attention to any hesitancy that you have when pondering your response to God during oratio. The work of idolatherapy applies during this step. Notice anything that makes you uncomfortable.

Ask yourself the following questions as you go deeper in your relationship with God:

What is keeping me from fully loving the God revealed in my reading?

How does the God revealed during lectio and meditatio contrast with my experience of God?

How does the text sound too good to be true?

What troubles me in the text that makes it difficult for me to articulate a soul response to God rather than merely a superficial or trivial one?

How does the tension between my experience and what the Scripture says feel in my body?

What other allegiances do I need to let go of or repent of in order to love God more authentically?

How does the text reveal any double mindedness or inner conflict within me?

Is there any aspect of the text that creates inner tension or guilt or shame? If so, what would it look like to surrender a little more deeply to God's grace right now and then praise God out of a deeper dependency on God's loving-kindness?

Notice how you feel after you reflect on loving God. Don't leave this step until you are at peace with the God who loves you.

The above questions are risky because they open us up to the transformational work that God desires to do in us. It can be painful initially and even scary to practice conscious transparency of our motives and inner struggles before God. But guess what? God already knows us inside and out. God waits for us to surrender the hurt, scared, and even sinful parts of ourselves to his loving light. As God once told Joshua:

> "Only be strong and very courageous, being careful to act in accordance with all the law that my servant Moses commanded you; do not turn from it to the right hand or to the left, so that you may be successful wherever you go. This book of the law shall not depart out of your mouth; you shall meditate on it day and night, so that you may be careful to act in accordance with all that is written in it. For then you shall make your way prosperous, and then you shall be successful." (Josh 1:7–8)

Contemplatio (contemplate). The second stage of application involves pondering how the text calls us to love others. Love for others flows out of an undivided love for God. We demonstrate our love for God by allowing God's love for us to flow freely to those around us, particularly to persons whom we may otherwise find difficult to love. Anyone can love those who love him or her first. It is the mark of perfection in love when we find it possible in our hearts to love even our enemies and those who trouble us. In our world that loves to call for justice, often we find an unwillingness to forgive others and sometimes outright malice toward persons who may disagree with us in the slightest.

The final step in lectio divina thus involves putting tangibly into action the ways that our text invites us to engage the world with the love of God.

Reflect on how the text imagines how we relate to brothers and sisters in Christ as well as to all souls living in the world. What does it mean to love my neighbor as myself based on my reading? How would I live differently in relationship according to the text I've been studying? What specific ways does my community of faith need to change in order to live out the ethic of the text? What is a tangible action that I can take today to begin to make the ideals in the text more concrete in my life and in how I engage the world?

Into the World

Before completing your study time, reflect for a few minutes on your goal of engaging Scripture. We wrestle with the text to gain its word of blessing so that we can then realign with it and share it with others.

Spend a few minutes pondering and praying for guidance on a small step that you can take even today with what God taught you during your reading time. Perhaps even sit in silence for a few moments to digest the meal that God has provided you today.

Keep a personal journal available and simply spend 3–5 minutes writing down your thoughts to questions such as:

What did I learn today?

What are the deeper implications of what God has shown me?

What is keeping me from living out this word now?

How does this text challenge my present thinking and way of life?

How does this text affirm my present thinking and way of life?

What does this text invite me to care about?

What kind of person do I need to become to live out this lesson with integrity?

What is my plan for implementing my learning into tangible actions and habits in my daily life?

How can I share these ideas in ways that are inviting and transformational?

These questions are not meant to be exhaustive. But it is critical for your formation to not miss the opportunity for a deeper reflection into what the Spirit revealed to you.

Assignment for Reflection

Stop and spend 5 minutes in centering prayer and/or
journaling (see instructions above). Pick a favorite passage of
Scripture and apply the steps of lectio divina to it.

Suggested Resources for Going Deeper in Your Study of Scripture

A good study Bible with notes: *The Wesley Study Bible*, *NIV
Life Application Bible*, or Cultural Backgrounds Study Bible

A quality modern one-volume commentary on Scripture:

Wesley One Volume Commentary

The IVP Bible Background Commentary: Old Testament

The IVP Bible Background Commentary: New Testament

An up-to-date Bible dictionary:

Eerdmans Dictionary of the Bible

Advanced students (teachers/pastors) will want to supple-
ment the above with full scale commentaries.[52]

---

52   Portions of this chapter have been adapted from Brian D. Russell, "Conversa-
      tions with Scripture (1): Preparing Our Hearts and Minds," Catalyst, October
      3, 2016, https://www.catalystresources.org/preparing-our-hearts-and-minds-
      conversations-with-scripture/.

Chapter Fourteen:
New Questions and a Mindset for Transformation

Learning to read the Bible *for deep transformation* requires that we approach the text openhanded. As we learn to surrender more and more to the God who loves us, Scripture will be a principal means through which we hear God's voice. In this chapter, we'll explore key postures for listening and questions that, if asked, will deepen the lectio divina approach described in the previous chapter.

Mindsets for Deep Transformation

Scripture is not a magic book. Sometimes insight flows easily from its pages to our hearts and minds. Other times our reading may feel dry and even meaningless. As we've explored together, we have to be mindful of the subtle ways that we avoid the message of the Bible. Likewise, we need to put ourselves into intentional postures for receiving the good news.

Here are five mindsets that I've personally found helpful for reading Scripture in ways that grow me in love for God and neighbor.

1) Be open to being astonished and to hearing the voice of God. When we read Scripture, we engage the same sacred set of writings that faithful believers have read for more than two thousand years. As we've discussed, it is not enough to lift up Scripture as an authoritative artifact from the past. We need to approach our reading and reflection with an expectation of astonishment for the present moment. When Scripture astonishes us personally, we are ready to live and move in ways that will surprise the world with the love and grace of Jesus Christ. Also, I've found that when I've been astonished by the Word, I am more likely to help those whom I serve in my ministry to be astonished by God's love and grace as well. Let me remind you again of the prayer that helps me to enter into a space where I'm ready to receive all that God has for me. Pray: "Lord, astonish me anew with the riches and good news of your Word. Amen."

2) Approach the text as a learner rather than an expert. There is an irony in a lifelong reading of Scripture. Over time, texts become so familiar that we breeze through them assuming that we already know their message. Making this assumption is dangerous to our spiritual formation. It is likewise harmful to any other souls with whom we have the privilege of sharing the Word. What may be "old" news to us may be riveting news to another soul. Moreover, I've found that even familiar texts have hidden treasures for those who have eyes and ears to see and hear anew. It is therefore vital that we consciously avoid treating the text as an object over which we gain control via study. The moment that we reckon ourselves experts will mark the time when our voice becomes the authority rather than God's. Don't pray, "Lord, help me to master this text." Instead assume the posture of a learner and say, "Lord, I open myself to hear all that you have for me. Master me through my conversation with your Word."

3) Embrace listening over expecting immediate gratification. Our conversation with Scripture requires patient and persistent listening. We cannot control the speed of illumination and insight. Some passages will release their riches quickly and easily. Others will only do so slowly and with difficulty. In either case, we must be willing to be fully present with God and the text in a spirit of humility and dogged resilience. We cannot demand a word from God; we can only receive one gratefully with open hands, hearts, and minds. Remember the mark of the happy person in Psalm 1: he or she meditates on the Law of the Lord day and night (v. 2).

4) Practice radical openness with God through the text. We must be the first converts to any reading of the text. "The gospel comes to us on its way to someone else."[53] Resist the urge to make an application to someone else's life or situation until we've fully surrendered and embraced the text's message for us.

5) Align your mind, heart, and hands with the text, and take action. To listen to Scripture involves realigning with its message continually. Our conversation with Scripture must lead to tangible change and action. As James reminds us, "But be doers of the word and not merely hearers who deceive themselves. For if any are hearers of the word and not doers, they are like those who look at themselves in a mirror; for they look at themselves, and, on going away, immediately forget what they

---

53   This is one of my missional mentor Alex McManus's favorite sayings.

were like" (James 1:22–24). How do we become "doers"? We become doers by taking action based on our reading.

New Questions for Deepening Our Reading

How does this text teach me to pray?

How does this text challenge my current way of life as well as that of my community of faith?

What kind of person do I need to become to live out this text with integrity?

How does this passage stand in tension with my current thinking or understanding of the Gospel?

Who or what is this text calling me to care about?

What is one action that I must implement immediately according to this passage?

We cannot treat this stage as merely rhetorical. We need to write down or journal the key actions that we need to take. Then, go out and live the Gospel for the world.

Thank you, God, for the gift of Scripture. Give us the hearts and minds to listen and meditate on it so that we may encounter you, the living Lord of the text. Grant us the courage to dare to realign with its message and live it out before a world that desperately needs its good news. In Jesus' name, amen

Questions for Reflection

- Which of the above mindsets most resonated with you? Why?

- What do you sense are your present challenges to engaging with Scripture at a deep level?

Chapter Fifteen:
Sabbath and Work[54]

⸱⦿⸱

Thus the heavens and the earth were finished, and all their multitude. On the seventh day God finished the work that he had done, and he rested on the seventh day from all the work that he had done. So God blessed the seventh day and hallowed it, because on it God rested from all the work that he had done in creation.

(Genesis 2:1–3)

"Remember the Sabbath day, and keep it holy. Six days you shall labor and do all your work. But the seventh day is a Sabbath to the lord your God; you shall not do any work—you, your son or your daughter, your male or female slave, your livestock, or the alien resident in your towns. For in six days the lord made heaven and earth, the sea, and all that is in them, but rested the seventh day; therefore, the lord blessed the Sabbath day and consecrated it."

(Exodus 20:8–11; cf. Deut 5:12–15)

---

54 This chapter is based on an earlier essay that I published, "Sabbath and Work: Conversations with Scripture," Catalyst, June 12, 2017, http://www.catalystresources.org/sabbath-and-work-conversations-with-scripture/.

I'm always grateful for a question that stops me dead in my tracks. A couple of years ago, my then sixteen-year-old daughter asked me, "Dad, why do you work so much?" She had observed how fatigued I was driving home from work and asked this out of a deep concern for me. I had taken on multiple new roles and was struggling to juggle all of my responsibilities. My initial response was purely defensive: "To buy you all of the stuff that you ask me to purchase for you."

I quickly apologized, but I struggled to answer her question. My mind turned quickly to this: "I work so much because God wants me to." Those of us who live out our vocations as pastors, teachers, and religious professionals can easily mask over a compulsion to overwork by appealing to a sense of calling. But what happens when the work I believe I'm doing for God begins to feel like it's eroding the work that God desires to do in me? After all, workaholism is the one addiction for which a pastor will likely never be criticized.

The Bible's opening words challenge my assumptions about Christian calling, vocation, and work. Genesis 1:1–2:3 sets the tone and agenda for life as God intends. In sweeping language, this passage narrates God's effortless work of creation. God speaks all that is into existence over six days. Then God rests. The rest is called Sabbath. God embeds the rhythm of six days of work and one day of rest into the fabric of creation. God works. God rests.

Ponder the deep truth that the God who created the universe stitched rest into the fabric of our existence. But this reality is even better than you may think. When you have time, read Genesis 1:1–2:3 for yourself. You may notice some patterns. First, verse 2 begins with a description of chaotic beginnings. God does not begin with a clean and polished finished product. God begins with a chaotic mess that is formless, empty, and dark. But God's Spirit is there at the beginning. God hovers over the mess, poised and ready to act. This truth is a powerful reminder for all who seek out the God of Scripture. We do not have to appear before God at our best. We only have to open ourselves to God's work. In Genesis, God may begin with a raw collection of shapeless stuff, but God does not end there. God will transform this chaos into a very good world (1:31). The possibility of "very goodness" is true of our lives too. With God there is always hope for a beautiful tomorrow. We don't have to work our ways out of any mess or chaos in which we find ourselves. We simply need to *rest* in the trust and assurance that God is already present and ready to make "all things new" (Rev 21:5).

Second, the six days of creation unfold calmly and without drama. God's work appears almost effortless. There are no hiccups. There are no false starts. Everything goes as God intends. God simply imagines the elements of creation and speaks them into existence. All of us know that creative work of any kind is difficult. It is toilsome. It is tiring. Some great ideas take years or even a lifetime to ripen fully. But God makes it look easy in Genesis 1. Yet God still pauses to rest on the seventh day.

God does not keep on creating. God works for six days and then rests. God is powerful enough to make the work of creation seem simple but still takes Sabbath and embeds rest into the contours of creation. In its original setting, Genesis 1:1–2:3 is a declaration of God's reign over a creation that serves as

God's holy temple. In other words, the original readers would have understood the implication that God is a good King who reigns over a very good universe.

Third, the last act of creation before rest was the making of women and men to serve as image bearers of God to the rest of creation (1:26–31). Part of the work of image bearer is to serve as visible representatives of the invisible Creator God. The language of "be fruitful and multiply," "fill," and "have dominion" in 1:28 add an element of mission and intentional work for humans. God created humanity to be a community that fills all creation and reflects God's character. We can think of this as a priestly function. Humans are God's priests in God's holy temple, that is, creation. This vocation gains additional clarity in Genesis 2:15, "The lord God took the man and put him in the garden of Eden to till it and keep it." The language of "till and keep" implies creativity and cocreation. Humanity takes on the project of caring for and enhancing the good world that God has made. As Christians, we can also pick up Paul's language of "new creation" and "ambassadors" (see 2 Cor 5:17–20) to help us understand what it means to live as images of God. It is critical then to recognize that Genesis 2:1–3 is part of God's gift to humanity. The Sabbath is explicitly extended to people in the Ten Commandments (Exod 20:8–11; cf. Deut 5:12–15). God will even extend Sabbath rest to God's handiwork, including the land and the animal kingdom (Exod 20:8–11; 23:10–13).

Fourth, the work of creation advances from chaos and darkness to order, beauty, and light; from work to rest. This timing challenges our modern rhythms. We tend to think of a day as moving from day to night. Yet in Genesis the flow is this: "there was evening and there was morning" (1:5). Also, we often rest so that we can work. Instead, God models a vision of work that culminates in rest. These differences may appear subtle on the surface, but with reflection we find a radical challenge to our lives. Life is not a movement toward darkness or endless work. Existence moves toward light and rest. The future is better than the past. It is no coincidence that the biblical narrative as a whole begins with creation (Genesis 1–2) and concludes with a vision of New Creation (Revelation 21). Sabbath invites us to model the reality of New Creation in a world trapped in patterns that dehumanize and enthrone false gods rather than the true Creator. There is an inherent optimism in the biblical rhythms of life.

Finally, stepping back from the whole of Genesis 1:1–2:3, notice the overarching movement. In 1:2 we encounter a messy chaos. On days one to six God orders, shapes, and fills the created world. On days one to five God remarks that his work on each day is "good." So, on days one to five God moves creation from a messiness to a state of goodness. Then on day six God finishes God's work by filling the earth with all types of animals and then creates man and woman in God's image. At the end of day six, God evaluates the whole of creation as "very good" (1:31). So now creation has moved from a messy chaos to an "in process" goodness to a very good final product. But the good news gets better as Scripture announces something even better than "very good." This something is called Sabbath (2:1–3).

Sabbath is a space in which all striving and work cease. It is where our identity depends not on what we do or have done. Instead, our true identity is as men and women created in God's image. As such, God's love for us does not depend on any action we take or role we fill. The God of Scripture invites us to find true rest with and in his presence.

God reiterates the call to Sabbath through the rest of the Bible. Sabbath anchors the Ten Commandments (Exod 20:8–11; Deut 5:12–15) by bridging the commandments focused on God with the commandments focused on our relationships with others. The Torah's instructions on releasing slaves (Exod 21:1–11; Deut 15:12–18), caring for the land and animals (Exod 23:10–15), and forgiving debt (Deut 15:1–6) all find their roots in the Sabbath.

In the New Testament, Jesus extends the promise of Sabbath rest to his followers. Here is Jesus' invitation: "Come to me, all you that are weary and are carrying heavy burdens, and I will give you rest" (Matt 11:28). If Jesus offers his disciples rest, why do we often feel guilty for not working or simply ignore Jesus' invitation because we become so wrapped up in the roles we play in life?

Sometimes we justify our neglect of Sabbath rest by appealing to Jesus' actions. Since Jesus did good on the Sabbath and helped others, so should we. Some will cite Jesus' words in support of this: "The Sabbath was made for man, not man for the Sabbath. So the Son of Man is lord even of the Sabbath" (Mark 2:27–28 NIV), or "Is it lawful to do good or to do harm on the sabbath, to save life or to kill?" (Mark 3:4). In both contexts, Jesus is being provocative. Jesus did not break Sabbath in order to advocate for 24/7 ceaseless activity by his followers. Jesus broke Sabbath to prevent religious authorities from thwarting the true meaning of Sabbath by suffocating those most desperate for God. If we use Jesus' example to justify our lack of sabbath, we are missing the point.

I continue to ponder my daughter's question. If God, who effortlessly created this universe through words alone, modeled rest on the seventh day, why do I feel the need to work so much?

Given what Scripture teaches, I cannot appeal to my calling to justify overwork. Perhaps my desire to overwork and avoid Sabbath points to a deeper truth. Maybe I feel that I have something to prove. Maybe it's to cover up the dull ache on the inside that reminds me of past failings, disappointments, or regrets? Is it a deep longing for absolute certainty and security that depends more on my abilities and strengths (or lack thereof) apart from a deep trust in God? Or maybe it's simply that I don't believe I'm enough and therefore have to earn grace and love?

Since Scripture's consistent witness points to the importance of Sabbath rest, reading these texts leads me to lean even deeper into my love for God by receiving the gift of Sabbath with open hands. I can simply stop for a day each week any activity that I do for monetary gain or for personal achievement. Such activities include work done in the name of God.

Will there ever be time to shorten a Sabbath rest for the sake of serving and blessing those in need? Of course, but such occasions need to be rare. Otherwise, I am likely deceiving myself and modeling for others a self-made life rather than a life truly dependent on God.

I can give thanks to God for inviting me into an intentional pause so that I can *remember* who I am and whose I am. I can surrender a little more because I know that I am safe in the God who loves me. I let go of work or a fear of lack because I know that in Christ, I am enough. Since I am enough, I can let go of any actions driven by my ego needs or by the "should" imposed on me by others. I can be still and know that Jesus Christ is Lord and bask in God's love as a means of being able to extend that love to the world.

Thus, the call of Sabbath also points us to loving others. Sabbath is never about me alone. Sabbath is for all creation. Even the Creator paused on the seventh day. The challenge of a biblical Sabbath is that it is communal. I cannot take sabbath and then cause another to break his or her Sabbath on my behalf. Such a statement creates some challenges because the days of a society-wide Sabbath have been over since ancient times. Yet the fact that the Sabbath commandment is the longest of the ten commands suggests that God's people have always tended to look for loopholes. Read over the long list of reminders in the commandment itself. I can't expect another person—even a servant—to work in my place. Even work animals are awarded Sabbath rest.

Some communities of faith, especially those in the Adventist tribes, still practice a communal Sabbath. My own sense of the importance of sabbath today was influenced by some Adventist students in my earliest days of teaching. I'm not advocating any particular Sabbath practice other than to remind us that we are not honoring the spirit of Sabbath if we don't support a Sabbath rest for those around us too.

Moreover, the application of Sabbath in ancient Israel to issues of crop rotation, debt relief, and emancipation reminds us that Sabbath has justice embedded in it. Part of our larger life outside of Sabbath involves actively taking action to do good for others and avoiding practices that harm others. Also in our modern economies, we struggle with unemployment and underemployment as well as with persons who are not interested in working at all. Sabbath invites us to give pause in order to ponder how best to honor our Creator by finding ways to love our neighbors in these various places in life.

> How can I rest today so that I can love my brothers and sisters more authentically over the long haul of life?
>
> How can I enjoy the abundance of this present moment with God as a way to witness to the "enoughness" of God's provisions for me?

These questions bring me back to the opening chapter of Genesis again. God began with a mess, brought it to very goodness, and then added rest on the other side of very goodness.

What if Genesis 1:1–2:3 is not merely a story about creation? Instead, what if it's an invitation to true life and rest? Maybe Scripture wants to tell me that God is enough for me and I am enough for God. Maybe then I'll find the rest and abundance that God has offered us from the beginning. What do you think? Will you join me in finding out?

Questions for Reflection

Spend a few minutes answering the questions posed above. Focus on either carving out time for Sabbath or, if you consistently practice Sabbath, pondering how you can enhance your present times of Sabbath so that they become truly soul-enhancing times.

- What are your main takeaways from our study of Sabbath?

- How do Genesis 2:1–3 and Exodus 20:8–11 shape you to love God and neighbor?

Chapter Sixteen:
Is God on My Side?
Reading Joshua 5:13-15[55]

Once when Joshua was by Jericho, he looked up and saw a man standing before him with a drawn sword in his hand. Joshua went to him and said to him, "Are you one of us, or one of our adversaries?" He replied, "Neither; but as commander of the army of the lord I have now come." And Joshua fell on his face to the earth and worshiped, and he said to him, "What do you command your servant, my lord?" The commander of the army of the lord said to Joshua, "Remove the sandals from your feet, for the place where you stand is holy." And Joshua did so.

(Joshua 5:13–15)

In a world rife with division, uncertainty, anxiety, and tension, the desire for clarity and certainty is strong. Culture

---

55   I dedicate this chapter to my teacher and mentor Dr. John Oswalt, who first introduced me to Joshua 5:13–15 in a small group discipleship setting at Asbury Seminary in the mid-1990s.

wars rage as ideologies and religious convictions compete for dominance. The temptation for followers of Jesus is to play the same power games as the world. Our commitments to God can be co-opted so that rather than serving God we live as though God serves us. Moreover, we can create a false binary between ourselves as God's people and other souls whom God has called us to serve and bless in anticipation of them following the way of Jesus.

As we prepare for faithful mission in our communities today, we need to get clear on a fundamental lesson and posture for living as the people God has called us to be. It's a countercultural truth. The great impediment to our future isn't something outside of ourselves; it's our inner desire for certainty and control especially during difficult seasons of life.

In Joshua 5:13–15, Joshua has a high-altitude encounter with God that solidifies his formation as a spiritual leader. The same lesson learned by Joshua is critical for each of us to ponder and embrace. All of Joshua 5 records Israel's preparation for inhabiting the land God first promised to Abram and Sarai (Genesis 12). Now the hour of fulfillment has arrived. The book of Joshua is messy to read. It is full of violence and of what some might call "genocide" or "ethnic cleansing."[56] But a closer reading offers a more nuanced story. Israel is not a superpower bullying a smaller nation. Israel is the underdog in the wider Old Testament world. God's people succeeded by the grace of

---

56 It is beyond the scope of these pages to do a deep dive into these challenges. For additional reading on the topic, I recommend three resources that may be helpful: Christopher Wright, *The God I Don't Understand: Reflections on Tough Questions of Faith* (Grand Rapids: Zondervan, 2008); Stanley Gundry, *Show Them No Mercy: Four Views of God and Canaanite Genocide* (Grand Rapids: Zondervan: 2003); and Walter Moberly, *Old Testament Theology* (pp. 41–74).

God. Israel's security was never found in its military might or inherent wealth. In Joshua 3–4, Israel successfully crossed the river Jordan into the promised land of Canaan by miraculous means. God dammed the river so that they could cross through on dry land just as God created a pathway through the Red Sea a generation earlier (Exodus 14). A military vanguard did not secure the crossing; priests and Levites did by carrying the Ark of God's presence.

As Israel prepared to face the mighty Canaanites, the Lord ordered Joshua to lead the people in a series of religious rituals to prepare for the campaign ahead. Fascinatingly, none of the preparation involved the sorts of drills or instructions used by armies today. Nor do we find any record of stockpiling weapons or supplies. In fact, the supply of manna stopped during this time (Josh 5:12).

Instead, Israel's preparation was *spiritual* and *communal*. First, God ordered the Israelite men to be circumcised (Josh 5:1–9). Ouch. I'm certain that no other male warriors in history prepared for battle by cutting off their foreskins. But this action solidified their position as God's people descended from Abram. The act of circumcision initiated them into the people of God and thus heirs to God's promises. Second, God's people celebrated the Passover on the plains of Jericho. Passover was the means of remembering the mighty acts of deliverance by which God freed Israel from bondage in Egypt (Exod 12:1–13:16) and freed them for God's mission in the world (Exod 19:3–6). Passover served also to teach God's people about their true identity and shaped them into a community of blessing in the world. As followers of Jesus, we likewise practice these same rituals today in the new form of baptism (initiation) and the Lord's Supper (remembrance, identity, and mission).

When the stakes are highest, God's people do not rely on human tactics or ingenuity but on God. Joshua will lead God's people into the land, but it is God who makes the way.

While near Jericho (presumably scouting to prepare for the coming conflict with the Canaanites in the area), Joshua encounters a man standing before him with a drawn sword. Joshua asks an obvious question: "Are you one of us, or one of our adversaries?" (5:14).

The man responds, "Neither." An alternative translation would be simply "No" or "Not." In other words, it's the wrong question.

We live in a world marked by division. But God's mission isn't about exclusion and taking sides. It's about blessing all nations (Gen 12:3, Exod 19:5–6, Matt 28:18–20, John 3:16, 2 Cor 5:17–20). The Gospel is God's *yes* to the world. God's people are agents of God's abundance, not merely to those who already know and love God but even to those whom others may consider enemies. Jesus called his followers to a life of perfection in love: "Be perfect, therefore, as your heavenly Father is perfect" (Matt 5:48). The immediate context of Jesus' teaching (Matt 5:43–48) offers God as the example in terms of the sun rising on the good and bad and sending rain for both the just and the unjust. The Jesus-loving response to a world that desires division is "Love your enemies and pray for those who persecute you" (5:44).

Joshua asked his question innocently, but God still needed to correct him. The true question isn't, "Is God on *my* side?"

God doesn't take the sides of humans. The God of Scripture is radically for all people. God loves the whole world (John 3:16). The right question that we need to ask is this: "Am I or are we on God's side?"

Human history is littered with the wreckage that occurs when one people believe that they can act *for* God. To think that we ever know enough to be 100 percent certain that we are fully in the right is naive at best. And as history shows repeatedly, this assumption is *murderous* and *genocidal* at worst. Aleksandr Solzhenitsyn in his sublime *Gulag Archipelago* observed this truth about the delusion of being on the *right* side of any issue: "If only it were all so simple! If only there were evil people somewhere insidiously committing evil deeds, and it were necessary only to separate them from the rest of us and destroy them. But the line dividing good and evil cuts through the heart of every human being. And who is willing to destroy a piece of his own heart?"[57]

In Joshua 5:14, the man immediately self-identifies as "commander of the army of the lord" who has "now come." In other words, Joshua isn't standing before a mere mortal. This figure is an angelic being or perhaps even a theophany.[58] Whether the "man" is an angelic messenger or God in the appearance of a human matters little. Joshua is fundamentally in the presence of the Divine.

Joshua's response is an immediate surrender. The figure has a drawn sword, but Joshua goes face-first into the ground into a posture of submission and worship. His life is for the taking.

---

57 Aleksandr Solzhenitsyn, *Gulag Archipelago*, 168.
58 John Wesley believed this figure to be the Son of God.

There is a fundamental shift in Joshua. He moves from *willfulness* to *willingness*. Don't be fooled by the similarity of these two words. The moment we move from self-will (willfulness) to an openhanded surrender (willingness), God no longer has to work *against* our hardened hearts. The Spirit can flow freely into the area of low pressure created by our surrender. A surrendered life is the doorway to living fully for the love of God and neighbor.

Joshua's words indicate the extent of the shift. He asks a question that opens him fully to the will of God (5:14): "What do you command your servant, my lord?" Notice the title that Joshua embraces. He self-identifies as "servant" for the first time. Previously in the book of Joshua, Moses was described as the servant of God (1:1, 2, 7, 13, and 15). Joshua had already been called to serve in Moses' role (1:1–9), but only now, in 5:14, does Joshua embrace the true status and identity of a person on the side of God.

Jesus reminds his disciples of the importance of embracing servanthood in Matthew 20:25–28:

> You know that the rulers of the Gentiles lord it over them, and their great ones are tyrants over them. It will not be so among you; but whoever wishes to be great among you must be your servant, and whoever wishes to be first among you must be your slave; just as the Son of Man came not to be served but to serve, and to give his life a ransom for many.

The Critical Need for Personal Holiness

But there is even more for Joshua. What does God order Joshua to do? The angel of the Lord simply commands Joshua to remove his sandals because Joshua is standing on holy ground.

God's response to Joshua is interesting in what it doesn't include. We see no battle plan for the coming campaign. In Joshua 1:1–9, the Lord has already assured Joshua of victory. Joshua simply needs to put his feet on the ground (1:3). Otherwise, his sole responsibility is to meditate on Scripture (1:8) and live out God's Word faithfully with resolve and courage (1:6–8). God has promised God's presence.

Instead of providing Joshua with a clear plan, God makes sure that Joshua has clarity about something even more critical: character. If Joshua is truly the servant of the Lord, then this reality must be reflected in Joshua's character. God is holy love. The lesson for us is clear. Our first responsibility as ones desiring to be God's hands, feet, and mouthpieces today is a commitment to a Christ like character, not the possession of a powerful plan.

Robert Murray M'Cheyne was a Scottish preacher who lived a short but significant life (1813–1843). He wrote the following words, "The greatest need of my people is my personal holiness. Take heed to yourself. Your own soul is your first and greatest care. Keep up close communion with God. Study likeness to him in all things."

Joshua will face challenging days ahead, but Joshua represents one of the few authentically faithful and successful leaders of God's people in the Old Testament. Joshua and his generation succeeded in receiving God's gift of the land because they listened to and took action on the instruction of the Lord. Much of the rest of Israel's history (beginning immediately with the failures recorded in the book of Judges) is more a series of warnings about what unfaithfulness looks like. Joshua took God's call to holiness seriously and therefore remains a light to us today.

Let's ponder deeply how Joshua's sublime but odd encounter may manifest love for God and love for neighbor. First, loving God fundamentally involves our *willingness* to surrender our desire for clarity about long or short-term plans and focus on allowing God to work even more deeply within us. Our personal and corporate *transformation in love* is more important than our desire for control over our future.

Second, our perception of our enemies changes when we surrender to holiness. Yes, the violent aspects of the book of Joshua are difficult to read as moderns. But the truth is we remain surrounded by violence and the threat of violence today. We still see the extreme danger of warfare and tribalism. Violence always is just below the surface of our rhetoric, and it breaks out in a moment's notice. The violence in Joshua serves as a warning to us. Yes, our world is a dangerous place at times. We may be caught up in times of deep hostility and violence. Yet we must never imagine ourselves as somehow more godly or more worthy of God's love than those who may oppose us. In fact, Joshua's encounter with the divine ought to give us pause before unilaterally assuming that those who oppose us are the enemies of God. The book of Joshua gives indication that there was never a "black and white" or "us against them" certainty. Some Canaanites, including inhabitants of Jericho, became faithful Israelites. Rahab, who ran a brothel, and her family received protection and joined Israel (Josh 2:1–24; 6:22–25). The Gibeonites (Joshua 9) likewise confessed their belief in the Lord (esp. Josh 9:9–12) and were spared. It is just as important to recognize that God's people were held to a higher standard. They failed to capture Ai despite the relative weakness of the city due to the sin of one person named Achan (Joshua 7). Israel as a whole would, centuries later, lose the land and be exiled to Babylon because of Israel's lack of faithfulness (Deut 28:15–68).

Third, Israel existed as God's missional people (Gen 12:3; Exod 19:4–6). They served as ambassadors of the true God in preparation for the coming of Jesus Christ. God was *for* Israel *for the sake of nations.* Even during times of struggle, it was never a matter of God being *against* others simply because they were not Israelites. All of God's actions paved the way for God's ultimate victory at the cross. Let us never forget that Jesus in his death rejected all forms of violent resistance and defeated sin, violence, political power, ideology, and even death through *surrender* to the divine will. Jesus' resurrection vindicated his model. We no longer have to live as Israelites who had at times to fight for a place in the world. Instead, we are now Christ's ambassadors in the world. Our weapons are faith, love, and hope. To resort to violence or even the demonization of the very persons for whom Christ died and continues to love is a denial of the Gospel itself. Joshua 5:13–15 invites us to ask, What kind of person do I need to become to surrender my need for God to be on my side and protect me from my perceived enemies?

The victories won by Joshua are in fact solely the work of God. God's people never win a single victory in their own strength. In fact, they *only* prevail when they live *faithfully* according to God's instructions.

What would it be like to be in the presence of that same angel of the Lord today?

Would I be willing to ask myself the hard question implicit in the angel's "No"?

Am I willing to ponder how I might not presently be on God's side?

Am I willing to consider that the soul whom I today consider my adversary may in fact be closer to the heart of God than I am?

Even if I discern my relative "rightness" in a matter, am I willing to put away my sword and extend a hand of fellowship as a means of extending love to the "other"?

Am I willing to lose myself if it means the greater long-term gain for the love of God in the world?

Lord, Jesus Christ, Son of God, have mercy on me a sinner. Amen.

Questions for Reflection

Reflect on the questions in the paragraph above. Then, answer the two below.

- What are your main takeaways from Joshua 5:13–15?

- How does it shape you to love God and neighbor?

Chapter Seventeen:
How to Pray the Psalms of Vengeance with Integrity

· • ● • ·

Psalm 137

By the rivers of Babylon—
there we sat down, and there we wept
when we remembered Zion.

On the willows there
we hung up our harps.

For there our captors
asked us for songs,
and our tormentors asked for mirth, saying,
"Sing us one of the songs of Zion!"

How could we sing the lord's song
in a foreign land?

If I forget you, O Jerusalem,
let my right hand wither!

Let my tongue cling to the roof of my mouth,
if I do not remember you,
if I do not set Jerusalem
above my highest joy.

Remember, O lord, against the Edomites
the day of Jerusalem's fall,
how they said, "Tear it down! Tear it down!
Down to its foundations!"

O daughter Babylon, you devastator!
Happy shall they be who pay you back
what you have done to us!

Happy shall they be who take your little ones
and dash them against the rock!

Has the idea of praising God ever felt oppressive to you? It is popular in some churches to use the following call and response in worship services:

God is good. All the time
All the time. God is good.

How did it feel for you to read these words? Do they really resonate with your experience?

It may depend on the meaning of resonate. Many of us believe that God is good. It's a central theme of the Christian understanding of God. But I've sat in enough worship services where I've seen people weep, remain tight-lipped, or even put their heads down in sadness when these words (or similar ones) are spoken. During a dark season of my life, I found the refrain suffocating rather than liberating.

So, can praise ever feel oppressive? Yes, at times it can. Of course, we all would likely prefer a feel-good faith with happy endings and smiles. Some of us do enjoy a relatively pleasant life, but Psalm 137 exists to remind us of the harsh realities for some of God's people. Psalm 137:9 contains one of the most offensive and disturbing affirmations in the Bible. This verse is a prayer of blessing for a hoped-for atrocity. It is indeed envisioning an unspeakable act against innocent infants. What is it even doing in our Bible? How can any *decent* person ever pray such words? What does a prayer for vengeance against the children of enemies have to do with the double love of God and neighbor?

Most who read this book likely live in the sanitized Western world and have not experienced the type of war crime described in Psalm 137. Yet the trauma of personal violence and abuse may still reside deep in us. Emerging generations suffer high rates of depression. Teen suicide is high. Significant percentages of adults have suffered sexual trauma. Millions of children grow up in homes without two loving parents, scarred by issues of abandonment or the repercussions of divorce. The year 2020 brought to the forefront the trauma of African Americans caused by generations of suffering the effects of racial injustice. The isolation of the COVID-19 pandemic led to increased anxiety, stress, and fear.

Pain creates blocks to an abundant future.[59] Pain and trauma can mute the good news of the Gospel in our lives. In

---

59 See Bessel van der Kolk, *The Body Keeps the Score: Brain, Mind, and Body in the Healing of Trauma* (New York: Penguin Books, 2014).

parts 1 and 2 of this book, we explored conscious and unconscious blocks that we bring to our study of the Bible. Often our readings of Scripture inadvertently oppress the very persons who need the healing and balm of God's love.

I've experienced the oppressive nature of a feel-good faith. In the years following my 2011 divorce, I struggled with attending church services. The problem wasn't the message of the Gospel. The problem was my pain. The hurt inside created blocks to my two previous favorite parts of worship services: the singing and the sermon.

I was unable to sing for several years because my heart was still aching from my wounds. I found most modern praise songs to be out of touch with my pain. Don't get me wrong. I love music. I even intellectually appreciate the lyrics. But chorus after chorus of "How Great Is Our God" or "What a Wonderful Name It Is" created a tension in my bones because I could not sing those words with integrity due to my pain. These songs championed a powerful God who did great things. The message simply did not ring true for me at an existential level during that season. Believe me: I wanted it to be true. I wanted my life to have a happy ending. I desired to see the pain of my daughters assuaged. I wanted the mountain of debt from lawyer fees and court costs erased. I'd followed Jesus since my youth. I'd lived my life sacrificially. I did my best to treat others well. I lived generously. But I had suffered a great wound that singed my emotional core. The songs actually saddened me for a season and even caused me to question my own faith.

The sermons didn't help much either. I suddenly found most to be little more than poor imitations of popular self-help gurus or odd exhortations about issues that seemed irrelevant to my personal experience. Please don't read the above as criticism of the local church or pastors. I write these words simply to name realities that I know are not unique to me. There will always be souls in our communities of faith whose experiences mirror mine. This book is a testimony to the ongoing work that God's done in my life. Psalms such as Psalm 137 have been important in the healing of my heart. I want to suggest that Psalm 137 and similar laments are the friends of anyone who struggles with past pain.

Psalm 137 and Rage

First, let's be clear about one thing. Psalm 137 is not encouraging human violence against others. There is no message here about taking vengeance into our own hands. Second, it is critical to understand the context and its intent. It can be misused by both the powerful and the powerless.

Psalm 137 is not a prayer for the powerful. The powerful will never need such a prayer. When I was younger, I foolishly read Psalm 137 in worship on the Sunday following the 9/11 attacks on the United States. I naively equated the United States (the only superpower at that time) with ancient Israel. Israel was never a world power. I'm not suggesting that the pain and trauma of 9/11 did not require serious reflection and healing. I'm also not implying that acts of terror such as done on 9/11 do not require a military or police response. The innocent do indeed deserve protection wherever they live in the world. But the truth of the matter is that the United States took revenge against those responsible for 9/11 and didn't need God's help to do so given the vast military resources at its disposal.

Psalm 137 is a prayer of the powerless. To pray Psalm 137 with integrity means that you don't have any power. You have been victimized and can't seek out revenge even if you wanted to. For the powerless, Psalm 137 gives voice and invites victims of atrocities to name their pain *and* give it to God. The brutality of Psalm 137:9 involves relinquishing personal vengeance by handing the desire to God.

But Psalm 137 also has a warning for the powerless. Don't *revel* or *live* in the rage. *Relinquish* it and allow God into those places of *pain*. To pray words like Psalm 137 takes courage. It is not easy to own one's feelings of rage and desire for vengeance. But to keep it bottled up is even worse. Moreover, it also requires courage to surrender our natural inclination to seek personal revenge against those who have hurt us deeply.

Capturing the Rage

We already explored how praise can sometimes feel oppressive. Now let's explore another question that Psalm 137 raises: If praise can sometimes feel oppressive, can rage sometimes help us heal? Let me take you on a quick journey through the book of Psalms to provide some context for reading Psalm 137.

The psalms form us for the journey of life. The psalms are God's gift to God's people and serve as our prayerbook for living out God's mission. Yet the psalms can jar us with the raw emotion that pours out of them. We have a tendency in the modern church to gravitate to their praises of God rather than their depiction of human pain. Who doesn't want to stand with the psalmist and sing "O Lord, our Lord, how majestic is your name in all the earth!" (Ps 8:1 NIV)? Or

> Your steadfast love, O lord, extends to the heavens,
>
> Your faithfulness to the clouds,
>
> Your righteousness is like the mighty mountains,
>
> Your judgments are like the great deep;
>
> You save humans and animals alike, O lord. (Ps 36:5–6)

But we can't cherry-pick the psalms any more than we can cherry-pick our life's experiences. Enter Psalm 137. Let's explore where it falls in the book of Psalms. Beginning with Psalm 90, the Psalter begins a final movement to its climax of praise: "Let everything that has breath praise the lord" (Ps 150:6 NIV).

Psalms 88–89 conclude the Psalter's Third Book (Pss 73–89) with two poignant laments about individual and national loss. God's people have been exiled, and silence and darkness loom. Psalms 88–89 seem to lack hope. How will God's people move forward in light of the disaster of exile? Who will be their king now that the Davidic monarchy has apparently ended? But there is always a way forward with God. What does the future look like for God's people?

Fascinatingly, Psalm 90 is the only psalm linked to Moses. God's people can move forward by rediscovering their roots in Moses. Moreover, Psalms 90–100 reanchor God's people in the true security of God as King. Human kings may come and go, but the Lord reigns forever (e.g., Ps 93:1–2).

Psalms 100–106 worship God for his steadfast love and re-commit God's people to faithfulness. Psalms 107–18 continue to celebrate God's steadfast love and focus particular attention on God's great act of salvation in the Exodus from Egypt. Psalm 119 anchors faithfulness in a moment-by-moment relation-ship with the Lord through a scripture-centered piety: "Your word is a lamp to my feet and a light to (per NRSV) my path" (119:105). Then we have the songs of Ascent, 120–134, where we discover a collection of psalms written to serve pilgrims on their way to worship in Jerusalem. They are a celebration of faith, security, and community.

Psalms 135 and 136 celebrate God's saving history and his eternal goodness rooted in God's faithful action in Israel's history. Consider for example the constant refrain that opens Psalm 136 and then repeats throughout its rendition of history: "O give thanks to the lord, for he is good, for his steadfast love endures forever." Is not this language the origin of our modern saying "God is good all the time. All the time God is good"?

Moreover, notice how Psalm 136 ends. It moves from a survey of all of the miraculous acts of God (vv. 1–22) to an affirmation of God's work in the present (vv. 23–25):

It is he who remembered us in our low estate,

for his steadfast love endures forever;

and rescued us from our foes,

for his steadfast love endures forever;

who gives food to all flesh,

    for his steadfast love endures forever.

I love the praise and message of Psalm 136. But there is an important question that sits just under the surface of the certainty expressed. What about those who suffer and do not experience God's care in their "low estate"? What about the ones whom God didn't rescue from foes? What about the animals and even children who go to bed hungry and those who die of starvation in our world? Psalm 137 is for them. I believe it follows the happy Psalm 136 for the sake of balance.

I always imagine an older couple sitting in the corner of a worship service. It's testimony time. Everyone is praising God for how all of their needs are met daily. The old couple nods at one another before the husband speaks up about the significant challenges in their life. They had lost a child due to a hit-and-run. The husband served in the armed forces and had experienced firsthand the horrors of war and continues to struggle from the trauma of it. The wife has her wounds too, but she's not able to open up fully about her life. They aren't killjoys. They haven't lost all faith. They simply steadfastly refuse to whitewash their experiences of pain.

In our congregations, there will always be souls who have suffered. The Church at its best offers safety and a place to heal. But the danger is the temptation to proclaim a feel-good faith that papers over pain, or to project from the front stage images of beauty and success, over deep substance.

I think that Psalm 137 exists as authoritative Scripture to serve as a reminder of the darkness that lurks under the surface of our world. When we read Psalm 137, its words confront us about pain, evil, suffering, and the desire for retribution and justice by those who've faced the horrors of human existence.

Psalm 137 steadfastly refuses to whitewash the past or to create a false narrative that believes naively that positive feel-good praise can erase the pain of an individual or community. Our pain will inevitably squirt out and distort other areas of our life as well as our witness if we do not confront it. In his epic *The Gulag Archipelago*, Solzenitsyn shared this Russian proverb while recounting the atrocities of the Soviet labor camps: "Dwell on the past and you'll lose an eye. Forget the past and you'll lose both eyes."[60] It is better to name our pain than to suppress it and pretend as though it has no bearing on our present.

What happens when we offer a whitewashed and feel-good faith apart from pain? It creates profound stress and a deep inner anxiety that alienates souls from God and others. I had a fascinating conversation with a middle-aged woman after a yoga class a few years ago. She had shared with us that her intention that day was to remember her dog, who had just died. I was a couple of mats over, so when we finished, I simply expressed my condolences to her. She then said, "You seem like a spiritual man. I can sense kindness in you." She went on to share that the death of her pet was just a sample of her pain. Her husband had divorced her and left her struggling financially. She had to move to make ends meet and had few friends. Now she was also facing unemployment.

---

60   Aleksandr Solzhenitsyn, *The Gulag Archipelago 1918–56: An Experiment in Literary Investigation,* abridged and introduced by Edward Ericson Jr. (London: Vintage, 1985), xxxii.

I asked, "Where are you in your spirituality? Do you have any sort of relationship with God or support from a faith community?"

"No, in fact, I'd like to tell God to 'f—k off.'"

I replied, "Oh, so you do have a relationship with God?"

"No, I just told you I'd tell him to 'f—k off.'"

"Sorry. That sounded like a prayer to me. The God I believe in is big enough to handle all your pain and your hurt."

"You mean I can really say how I feel to God? I've never been to a church that taught me that."

"Why don't we pray right now?" I'll never forget this conversation. To be clear, I'm not suggesting that we encourage people to tell God to "f—k off." But by giving this woman permission to bare her soul before the God who loves her, I was able to witness to the God who inspired even texts such as Psalm 137.

Psalm 137 proclaims a deep faith. It is one that is steadfast to the core. It is a resilient faith. It will not submit to the empire that had destroyed Jerusalem and the Lord's temple, dehumanized God's people through violence and atrocity, and forced a migration to a foreign land.

The concluding three verses of Psalm 137 allow those who pray it to release rage, survivor's guilt, shame, humiliation, and thoughts of violent retribution. Any attempt to sanitize the viciousness of the last verse misses this key point. When powerless persons have experienced the unspeakable, they must be given voice to speak their pain, including thoughts of vengeance. But note that verse 9 is releasing the vengeance to another. Instead of plotting personal revenge, the pray-er presumably is handing over the responsibility for justice to God.

In modern societies, we establish laws and civil rights to protect the innocent and bring the perpetrators of evil to justice. But atrocities still happen. So, is Psalm 137 a model prayer for our daily devotions? Sometimes. Let's hope we never have to feel the extreme pain of the psalmist. But let's not forget that there are many in our world who do. Even if you can't relate to the trauma and victimhood present, praying Psalm 137 helps us to be mindful of persons who do. If we desire to serve as agents of blessing and ambassadors of God's abundance, we need to grasp the full spectrum of human life. Psalm 137 also reminds us to be patient with those in pain. It also warns us about oppressing them with a bumper-sticker faith.

Love for God and Neighbor (Even Our Enemies)

It is always important when reading any part of Scripture to ponder how it functions in its wider context. Above, I framed Psalm 137 as a counter-testimony against the praise of the psalms that preceded it. If we read Psalms 138 and 139, we gain additional insights into the power of Psalm 137.

In Psalm 138, the voice of David returns. Psalm 138 exhorts us to practice faithfulness even during difficult seasons. Verse 1 reads, "I give you thanks, O lord, with my whole heart; before the gods I sing your praise." The witness of Psalm 137 is that the possibility of a life of faithfulness abides even in the midst of unspeakable pain and exile. Psalm 137:3 portrays the Babylonians as tormenting God's people by asking them to sing a song about Zion from Babylon, the idea being that the Babylonians had reduced Zion to rubble and thereby demonstrated the powerlessness of Israel's God. Yet Psalm 138 declares the reality that the faithful can still sing God's praises as witnesses to the deepest truth even in the midst of other gods. So even the pain of Psalm 137 sets up those who pray it for *witness in the world.*

Psalm 137 expresses rage and the desire for vengeance, but as we continue to read Psalms 138 and 139, we also find an invitation for *continual growth, realignment, and purification.* God does not suppress our need to name our hurts. The temptation remains to set ourselves against the wicked without continuing our growth in love.

Psalm 139 contains some of the most familiar verses in the Psalter. Most of the psalm imagines an intimate relationship between the psalmist and God. For example, verses 13–14 read, "For it was you who formed my inward parts; you knit me together in my mother's womb. I praise you, for I am fearfully and wonderfully made. Wonderful are your works; that I know very well." Also popular are verses 23–24, "Search me, O God, and know my heart; test me and know my thoughts. See if there is any wicked way in me, and lead me in the way everlasting."

But contrast these verses with the tone of verses 19–22, where the same sort of desire for divine wrath we saw in Psalm 137 returns:

O that you would kill the wicked, O God,

and that the bloodthirsty would depart from me—

those who speak of you maliciously,

    and lift themselves up against you for evil!

Do I not hate those who hate you, O lord?

    And do I not loathe those who rise up against you?

I hate them with perfect hatred;

    I count them my enemies.

Note the overall message within Psalm 139. To proclaim one's loyalty and set oneself apart from the wicked *assumes* that one is walking with integrity and clean hands. Verses 23–24 serve as a model prayer for us as we seek to represent the way of Jesus today. Once we've felt the rage of psalms like 137 and 139, we are open to reflect and receive the good that God offers. The goodness of God involves transforming us into persons who are freed to love others, even our persecutors.

For me the model of deep transformation is seen on the Cross, where Jesus is able to extend forgiveness to his executioners and abusers: "Father forgive them; for they do not know what they are doing" (Luke 23:34), and in the midst of his suffering still serve as an ambassador of the Gospel: "Truly I tell you, today you will be with me in Paradise" (v. 43).

How do we get there? It is the work of grace, but Psalm 137 points the way. Psalm 137 teaches us to love God enough to surrender even our deepest pain in prayer. Psalm 137 then also models a way to love our neighbor, even our enemies, enough to put away our sword and refuse the way of violent retribution. This transformation begins by giving voice to those who have suffered greatly.

Surrendering deep trauma to God and learning to love our enemies and even pray for them are not easy actions. They are the result of a ripening faith that continues to pray, "Search me, O God, and know my heart; test me and know my thoughts. See if there is any wicked way in me and lead me in the way everlasting."

What kind of person do I have to be or become in order to be able to pray Psalm 137 with integrity? Am I ready to allow God to search and know my heart?

Questions for Reflection

Answer the questions in the prior paragraph.

- What are your main takeaways from Psalm 137?

- What does even a psalm of extreme violence and vengeance teach us about the love of God and neighbor (even our enemies)?

Chapter Eighteen:
Skin in the Game

————— · ◦●◦ · —————

Brothers and sisters, join in imitating me, and observe those
who live according to the example you have in us.

(Philippians 3:17)

What kind of person do I need to become to serve as a model
of Christ like character for others? I love this question because
it's evergreen. There is always more room for growth in love for
God and neighbor. As we allow the Holy Spirit to do its work
of idolatherapy in our lives, we'll discover that growth in grace
is an infinite game. The question isn't: Am I there yet? Instead,
it's: How far along the road can I get?

I took up surfing in my late thirties. I'd been watching surf-
ers from the safety of the seashore for years. I figured it was now
or never. My daughters were elementary school–age at the time.
They embraced the challenge with me. My progress was slow. It
took close to a hundred attempts before I ever caught my first

wave. Unlike her dad, my youngest was a natural. She was petite for her age. She was light enough that she didn't even need a full-sized board. She learned to ride on a four-foot body board.

She caught her first wave just south of Port Canaveral, Florida. We were maybe thirty yards offshore. She balanced on the body board while I held it steady. We patiently waited for the next set of waves. The perfect one arrived. I slid the board into the wave. My daughter kept her balance and glided down the face of the wave. At this moment, she did something extraordinary. She was so proud that while surfing the wave, she began announcing her triumph to everyone within earshot. She cried out, "Look at me! Everyone, look at me!"

I remember chuckling about her public display of pride and thinking that she'd grow out of it. Yet, while reading Paul's letter to the Philippians, Paul's words in 3:17 reminded me of my daughter's words. Let's look at it again: "Brothers and sisters, join in imitating me, and observe those who live according to the example you have in us."

In other words, Paul was saying: "Friends, look at me." Or perhaps more pointedly: "Friends, if you want to see what a Christ-centered life looks like, watch me and model your life accordingly." Wow. What would it take for you, my dear reader, and me to root ourselves so deeply in Christ that we can say Paul's words to one another with integrity?

In Philippians, Paul calls the believers in Philippi to live as citizens worthy of the Gospel of Christ (1:27–30; 3:20). Paul writes to empower Christ followers to serve as witnesses of the good news for their city. In Philippians, Paul offers four role models for Christian living. First, Paul begins with Jesus (2:1–18). He then reminds the Philippians of two leaders whom they knew personally: Timothy (2:19–24) and Epaphroditus (2:25–30). The latter was actually a Philippian believer. Then Paul offers his life as the final example (3:1–16).

The issue in Philippi was the status of the believers within the Roman world. Were they willing to fully embrace the Christian life when circumstances proved challenging? Many of the Christians in Philippi (like Paul himself) enjoyed Roman citizenship. Roman citizenship offered substantial privileges within the empire and was not common in the provinces. The city of Philippi was established as a Roman colony, so it enjoyed a standing that other cities outside of Rome did not. Those Philippian Christians with Roman citizenship therefore enjoyed privileges that their fellow believers around the Mediterranean world did not.

A fundamental insight in Philippians 1:27–4:1 is this: *the status that one embraces sets the limits of one's capacity to reach others with the Gospel.*[61] Roman citizenship offered a set of privileges that offered protections and benefits that one could exploit for his or her own benefit. In contrast, Paul sketches out a competing vision of being a citizen of heaven (1:27; 3:20). Unlike Roman citizenship, Gospel citizenship is rooted in a relationship with God through Jesus Christ. The Gospel citizen lays aside personal benefits and privileges for the sake of God's mission and for the good of others.

---

61 For a deeper exegetical dive into this statement and what follows, see my commentary on this text in *Wesley One Volume Commentary*, ed. Kenneth Collins and Robert Wall (Nashville: Abingdon, 2020), 799–805.

To illustrate this countercultural vision of citizenship, Paul begins with Jesus. When we think about models for Christian living, we always think of Jesus, right? We ask questions such as: What would Jesus do? Or what would Jesus say?

The hymn in Philippians 2:6–11 about Jesus' incarnation, crucifixion, and exaltation captures the core message about how a citizen of heaven lives. Verse 2:6 begins with a powerful statement: although (or perhaps because) Jesus shared equality with God, he did not exploit his high status for his personal gain. In the Roman world of scarcity and pure power, the exploitation of status was a given. How else can I get ahead in life if I do not take advantage of my privilege? Instead, Jesus renounced the status and privileges of divinity and embraced the status of a slave (2:7). By embracing the status of a slave, Jesus flipped the script on the Roman social ladder. Slaves were at the bottom, far below the gods as well as below the status of a Roman citizen. In fact, Jesus embraced his slave status to the extent that he became obedient to death on a cross (2:8). Don't miss the significance of this statement. Jesus could have died in a variety of ways to atone for sin. But he took up the cross in part because crucifixion was reserved for those of no status, such as slaves. Yet what happened to Jesus (2:9–11)? God highly exalted him and gave him the name above all names.

This subversive action by Jesus is the first model for what a citizen of heaven looks like. The Philippians were to work out their salvation (2:12) in light of Jesus' life and shine as stars within their generation (2:15).

It is always easy to point to Jesus as the model. He is God, after all. Moreover, Jesus is no longer physically present. Thus, we can view his story as more aspirational than attempt to embody it fully. We can express a desire to live like Jesus, but I've noticed that it's all too easy to settle for something less. We are only human after all. But Paul immediately challenges this assumption.

Paul moves to include three persons whom the Philippians knew intimately as contemporary examples of Christ like character and action: Timothy (1:1; 2:19–24), Epaphroditus (2:25–30), and himself (1:1–26; 3:1–16). Timothy demonstrated a genuine other-centered outlook in the way that he ministered among the Philippians. Epaphroditus was a member of the Philippian community. He faced death in order to serve in the mission of the Gospel when the Philippians sent him to help the imprisoned Paul. Paul himself suffered in prison (1:12–26) and modeled the reality that knowing Christ Jesus as Lord was a greater gain than any mere human accomplishment (3:1–16).

The Philippians knew these men. Paul couldn't distort their character or accomplishments. Paul took this risk to teach us the importance of our personal lives in the advance of the Gospel. Paul could say with integrity, "If you want to see what a Jesus-centered life looks like, look at me as well as the lives of my coworkers, Timothy and Epaphroditus."

Philippians 3:17 calls us to remember and give thanks for the women and men in our lives from whom we've learned how to live out the life of Jesus in our day. More importantly, it challenges us to recognize the necessity of nurturing our holiness as an integral part of how God advances his mission in the world.

Paul's vision of a Gospel citizenship invites us to praise the Lord Jesus for modeling a truly prosperous life by undercutting the power dynamics of the world. God grants Jesus the "name above all names" because Jesus embraced servanthood. I can love and worship a god who doesn't merely demand obedience because of his power and status. I get to worship the Lord of the universe, who has "skin in the game." As the writer of the Hebrews later penned: "For we do not have a high priest who is unable to sympathize with our weaknesses, but we have one who in every respect has been tested as we are, yet without sin. Let us therefore approach the throne of grace with boldness, so that we may receive mercy and find grace to help in time of need" (Hebrews 4:15–16).

George Orwell in his classic *Animal Farm* critiqued revolutionary movements for their cynical top-down authoritarianism that insulated their leaders from the lived realities of their followers. Near the end of the book, a fundamental tenet of the revolution shifted from "All animals are equal" to "All animals are equal, but some are more equal than others."[62] The power of the biblical portrayal of Jesus is that he remains the "crucified one" (Mark 16:6). We love a God who modeled the life of faith to the point of death on a cross. Jesus does not reign over the universe merely as an omnipotent deity set apart from creation; he reigns as the living Lord who tasted death so that we likewise might become children of God.

Paul's vision for becoming a person worthy of imitation connects directly with growth in love for neighbor. The Christ-following movement is a community centered on Jesus.

---

62   George Orwell, *Animal Farm*, 50th Anniversary Edition with a preface by Russell Baker and introduction by C. M. Woodhouse (New York: Signet Books, 2004), 134.

The New Testament consistently uses the imagery of a body. Each of us plays a part. Just as Jesus modeled the need for actual skin in the game, so must we. But the type of life that Paul describes is about more than merely trying harder. It's about dying to self. Jesus embraced the cross and its shame despite the truth that he was God. Timothy, Epaphroditus, and Paul all in their individual ways did not cling to any particular rights or privileges. Instead, they surrendered to God's mission in the world. As I reflect on Paul's words, I'm reminded that I can love those around me more readily when I embrace a posture in which I surrender my need for status. I am enough in Christ so I can be a little less egocentric in my service to others.

When I die to self, I open up a little more to the deep work that God desires to do in me. I can begin to feel the force of Paul's language in Galatians 2:19–20: "I have been crucified with Christ; and it is no longer I who live, but it is Christ who lives in me. And the life I now live in the flesh I live by faith in the Son of God, who loved me and gave himself for me."

Ask: How might God be calling me today to surrender even deeper into the loves God and neighbor? The world is watching. The faith will not be won or lost on social media or even from the pulpits of faithful churches. My mentor Alex McManus used to say, "The Western world has lost its faith in the shadows of church steeples." We can argue about the truth of this statement, but it's hard to debate McManus on the follow-up that he gave: "But it will be rewon in the living rooms of faithful followers of Jesus." He wasn't giving an anti–organized church message. He was merely reminding us of the critical impact that we flesh-and-blood followers of Jesus have on the world through living out our faith before a watching world, especially before our neighbors, friends, coworkers, and families. When I use the expression "skin in the game," I'm talking about our lived faith in the world.

As he moves to conclude the book of Philippians, Paul returns to our theme one more time, writing, "Keep on doing the things that you have learned and received and heard and seen in me, and the God of peace will be with you" (4:9).

Ask: Who is watching, listening, and learning from me? As I think about Paul's words to the Philippians, I see and hear my daughter surfing and crying out, "Look at me! Everyone, look at me!" As I grow in grace, what kind of person do I need to become in order to serve as a model of Christ like character for others even more effectively tomorrow than I do today?

Questions for Reflection

Reflect on the questions in the above paragraph. Then, answer the two below.

- What are your main takeaways from Philippians 3:17?

- To whom may God be calling you to model the love of God and neighbor?

Conclusion:
Take Up and Read

Thank you for journeying with me all the way to the end of *Astonished by the Word*. The next step is putting into practice what you've learned. Be the wise builder that Jesus talked about at the conclusion of the Sermon on the Mount (Matt 7:24): "Everyone then who hears these words of mine and *acts* on them will be like a wise man who built his house on rock" (emphasis added). Pick up your Bible and recommit anew to allowing it to serve as a means of grace for your growth in love.

Let me summarize our journey with a simple statement: You must read Scripture. But you must equally allow Scripture to read you. I'm not suggesting that God's Word is lacking in power. It isn't. But it is not a *coercive* force.

Reading Scripture is a relationship. It's not a magic book that forces itself on us. As we've seen, the greatest impediment to Scripture's power is us. I believe that spending time consistently reading the Bible is a means of grace. But it is only a means of grace if we are open to receiving it as such.

Growth in love for God, neighbor, and self involves moving from grace to grace. Scripture as a means of grace also depends on our response. The key question that each of us must answer when reading Scripture is this: "Am I willing to receive the grace that God has for me in this text?" Or put another way, "Am I willing to allow this text to transform my life today?"

We spent our time reflecting on how to apply Augustine's teaching on biblical interpretation: "So anyone who thinks that he has understood the divine scriptures or any part of them but cannot by his understanding build up this double love of God and neighbor, has not yet succeeded in understanding them."[63]

Before he was the great theologian that we know today, he was a struggling soul. His conversion involved the first moment that he was truly astonished by the Word. At a pivotal time in his life, Augustine was in his yard, praying in desperation to God. He describes his experience in *Confessions*:

> I was asking myself these questions, weeping all the while with the most bitter sorrow in my heart, when all at once I heard the singsong voice of a child in a nearby house. Whether it was the voice of a boy or a girl I cannot say, but again and again it repeated the refrain "Take it and read, take it and read." At this I looked up, thinking hard whether there was any kind of game in which children used to chant words like these, but I could not remember ever hearing them before. I stemmed my flood of tears and stood up, telling myself that this could only be a divine command to open my

---

63   Augustine, *On Christian Teaching*, 27 (see intro., n. 1).

book of Scripture and read the first passage on which my eyes should fall.[64]

Augustine goes on to share that he walked back to where he had been conversing with his friend Alypius. He picked up a book of Paul's letters. He put his finger on a random passage and Paul's words transformed his life in that instant. Augustine had read Romans 13:13–14: "Let us live honorably as in the day, not in reveling and drunkenness, not in debauchery and licentiousness, not in quarreling and jealousy. Instead, put on the Lord Jesus Christ, and make no provision for the flesh, to gratify its desires." The Bible's story became Augustine's story. He grew to serve as one of the Church's great theologians and leaders.

Make a commitment to yourself and to God today that you will "take up and read" as Augustine once did. How do you make such a commitment? It's simple. You move past seeing Scripture as something you *should* do. Instead, you feel in your bones that a steady diet of God's Word is a *must* in your life.

Spend a few minutes right now reflecting on why Scripture is a must in your life. Who do you want to become? Then take up and read, my friend.

May the God of holy love astonish you with the riches of the Word and transform you so that you may embody love for God, neighbor, and self. Amen.

---

64   Saint Augustine, *Confessions*, bk.12, p. 177 (see chap. 9, n. 6).

Questions for Reflection

Take some time and look over your answers to the questions from previous chapters. Then, address the following:

- What are your main takeaways? How can you integrate these ideas into your daily life?

- Why is Scripture a must for you? How do you need to shift in order for Scripture to be a must?

- How would your life look and feel different if you leaned even deeper into growing in love for God and neighbor?

Connecting with the Author

Brian D. Russell, PhD, serves as a professor of biblical studies and as a coach for pastors and spiritually minded leaders. He is available in person and virtually for speaking, retreats, one-on-one mentoring, and group coaching.

Brian welcomes your questions, feedback, and stories regarding your deep reflection on Scripture and the process of spiritual growth.

Website
www.brianrussellphd.com

Email
Brian@brianrussellphd.com

Podcast:
The Deep Dive Spirituality Conversations
www.deepdivespirituality.podbean.com
Or search on your favorite source for podcasts

Social Media:
YouTube: www.youtube.com/deepdivespiritualitywithdrbrianrussell
Twitter: @briandrussell
Instagram: @yourprofessorforlife

Other Books by Brian Russell
Centering Prayer: Sitting Quietly in God's Presence Can Change Your Life (Paraclete, 2021).

(re)Aligning with God: Reading Scripture for Church and World (Cascade Books, 2016).

Invitation: A Bible Study to Begin With (Seedbed, 2015).

Printed in the USA
CPSIA information can be obtained
at www.ICGtesting.com
CBHW040312170324
5399CB00005B/7

9 781953 495730